Christmas
with Southern Living
1992

Compiled and Edited by
Vicki Ingham

Oxmoor House®

©1992 by Oxmoor House, Inc.
Book Division of Southern Progress Corporation
P.O. Box 2463, Birmingham, Alabama 35201

Southern Living is a federally registered trademark belonging to
Southern Living, Inc.

Library of Congress Catalog Card Number: 84-63032
ISBN: 0-8487-1091-6
ISSN: 0747-7791
Manufactured in the United States of America
First Printing

Editor-in-Chief: Nancy Janice Fitzpatrick
Director of Manufacturing: Jerry Higdon
Art Director: James Boone
Copy Chief: Mary Jean Haddin

Christmas with Southern Living 1992

Editor: Vicki L. Ingham
Assistant Editor: Dondra G. Parham
Contributing Editors: Heidi Tyline King,
  Margaret Allen Northen
Recipe Editor: Kaye Adams, Test Kitchens Director and Recipe
  Editor, *Southern Living* magazine
Editorial Assistants: Catherine S. Corbett, Karen Brechin
Assistant Copy Editor: Susan Smith Cheatham
Senior Photographer: John O'Hagan
Photostylist: Katie Stoddard
Production Manager: Rick Litton
Associate Production Manager: Theresa L. Beste
Production Assistant: Pam Bullock
Artists: Connie Formby, Steve Newman
Designer: Carol Middleton

To find out how you can order *Southern Living* magazine,
write to *Southern Living*, P.O. Box C-119, Birmingham, AL
35283.

Introduction 1

Christmas Around The South 2

A Gracious Welcome in Galveston 4
  The Moody Christmas Card Collection 9
Melrose Spins a Fascinating Tale 10
A Grand House for the Governor 14
Patrick Henry's Christmas 20
The Reindeer Are Racing
  in Houston 23

Holiday Traditions 25

Holiday Variety Is the Spice
  of Her Life 26
Cookies and Friends: The More,
  the Merrier 30
Two Hundred Thousand Ornaments,
  and Still Counting! 32
A Party with a Purpose 34
The Sweetest Lady in Town 37
  Elizabeth's Creamy Pulled Candy 37
Old-World Santas Carry Trinkets
  and Treasures 38
The Chrismon Tradition 40
  Cross-Stitched Chrismons 41
  Crocheted Chrismons 42

Contents

Decorating for The Holidays 43
Season's Greetings Start at the Door 44
How to Make a Beautiful Badge 48
Christmas "Under the Sea" 50
Display Poinsettias with Panache 53
A Southwest-Style Celebration .,., ... 54
Terrific Tablescapes to Create 58
  Marbleized Place Mats, Napkin Rings,
    and Candle Shades 62
  How to Marbleize 62
  Gold Lamé Roses 62
  Copper Candlesticks 63
  Copper Place Card Holders 64
  Copper Napkin Rings 64
A Tree That Glows 65
Beribboned Mantels 66
Crochet a Garland of Stars 68

Christmas Bazaar 69
Emboss Copper for Starry Frames 70
A Coppery Christmas 72
  Sponged Copper Tree 72
  Brass-and-Copper Wire Wreath 73
  Round Embossed Ornament 73
We've Put a Bunny on the Moon! 74
Clever Ideas for Recycling Christmas Cards 76
Craft Wise Men from Wood 78

Sculpt a Family of Carolers 80
Appliqué a "Sleepy Reindeer" Stocking 81
Knit a Pair of Feline Pals 82
Beaded Ornaments in
  Stained-Glass Colors 85
Woven Ribbons Make Keepsake
  Cookie Tins .,., ... 86
Perfect Pines on Hearts and Squares 88
  Ornaments 88
  Pine Tree Heart Pocket 89
Crochet a Stocking and Tree Skirt 90
  Stocking 92
  Tree Skirt 92
Smiling Eskimos for Earmuffs
  and Sweater 94
  Eskimo Sweater 94
  Eskimo Earmuffs 94
A Punched-Paper Card Sends
  a Lacy Greeting 96
Cinnamon Angels for Your Tree 97
Don Sequins and Beads
  for the Holidays 98

Celebrations from The Kitchen 99
Cookies Kids Love 100
  Teddy Bear Cookies 101
  Christmas Mice Cookies 101

Sweet Dreams, Chocolate Fantasies..........102
    Chocolate-Raspberry Roulage..............102
      Raspberry Sauce.........................103
    Cream-Filled Chocolate Cake..............104
      Cream Filling............................104
      Chocolate Frosting......................104
    Chocolate Bow...........................105
    Chocolate Paradise Pie..................105
    Chocolate-Candy Cheesecake..............105
    Chocolate-Mint Soufflé..................106
      Crème Fraîche Sauce.....................106
      Chocolate Pastries......................106
    Chocolate Tiramisu......................106
    Brownie Trifle..........................107
A Cocktail Buffet Makes
    Entertaining Easy.......................108
    Roast Beef Rolls with Lime-Jalapeño
      Mayonnaise.............................109
    Creamed Shrimp
      in Pastry Shells.......................110
    Rainbow Vegetable Tray..................110
    Black Bean Salsa........................110
    Fudge Bites.............................111
      Kahlúa Whipped Cream...................111
    White Chocolate Dip.....................111
    Cocktail Buffet Centerpiece.............112
Breads..114
    Wheat-Sour Cream Rolls..................115
    Ginger-Cheese Muffins...................116
    Tea Biscuits............................116
    Cherry-Butterscotch Ring................116
    Coffee Cake International................116
    Orange-Raisin Bread.....................117
    Cranberry Surprise Loaf.................117
    Golden Holiday Bread....................118
Confections.......................................119
    Peppermint-Chocolate Truffles...........119
    Peanut Butter Squares...................119
    Raspberry Divinity......................120
    Shortcut Pecan Pralines.................120
    Chocolava...............................120
    Apricot-Chocolate Chip Cookies..........121
    Apple Pie Bars..........................121
    Tiny Christmas Bites....................121
    Christmas Tree Sandwich Cookies.........123
    Shortbread Cookies......................123
Beverages...124
    Apricot Slush...........................124
    Cranberry Fruit Punch...................124

    Orange Punch............................124
    Santa's Quencher........................124
    Hot Buttered Coffee.....................124
    Brandy Cocoa............................124
    Icy Bourbon Tea.........................125
    Spirited Coffee Punch...................125
    Mocha Eggnog............................125
Desserts..126
    Raspberry-Beaujolais Sorbet.............126
    Lemon Mousse............................126
    Coconut Cream Cheesecake................127
    Strawberry-Glazed Christmas Cake........127
    Apple Lane Cake.........................128
      Apple Filling...........................128
      Boiled Frosting.........................128
    Southern Fruitcake......................128
    Cranberry Cake..........................129
      Orange Glaze............................129
    Apple Pie with Walnut Topping...........129
      Walnut Crumb Topping....................129
    Macadamia Pie...........................130
      Rum Syrup...............................130
    Caramel-Ice Cream Tart..................130
      Nutty Caramel Sauce.....................130
    Orange Dessert Cups.....................130
Gift Ideas..132
    Herbed Mayonnaise.......................133
    Jeweled Pepper Chutney..................133
    Herb Mix................................133
    Brandied Cheese Spread..................133
    Mustard-Garlic Marinade.................134
    Basil Jelly.............................134
    Snowflake Cupcakes......................134
    Lemon Poppyseed Cakes...................134
    Russian Tea Mix.........................135
    Chocolate Chip Pie Mix..................137
    Pumpkin Butter..........................137
Gifts Kids Can Make...............................138
    White Chocolate Crunch..................138
    Shortcut Gingerbread Cookies............138
    Edible Ornaments........................139
    Snack Mix...............................139
    Brown Sugar Brownie Mix.................139

Patterns...140

Contributors.....................................156

Introduction

Along with Santa's visit, Christmas dinner ranks high on the list of eagerly awaited holiday events. What better occasion, then, to lavish attention on creating a festive setting for food, family, and friends?

Little things that you might not ordinarily do can mark the gathering as special. For example, if you're seating eight or more guests, place cards are a thoughtful touch. And gearing table decorations and place settings to a theme instantly creates an atmosphere of celebration. Start with a single idea—say, using French horn ornaments as napkin rings. Paint a horn motif on the napkins, use hunting-horn ornaments for place card holders, sheet music for place mats, and French horns for the centerpiece—suddenly you've created a musical tablescape that will have your guests singing your praises!

One of the things you'll notice about many of the people featured in this year's book is the way they use themes to give a focus to their holiday traditions and decorations. A Baytown, Texas, grandmother keeps her children and grandchildren guessing as to what "Christmas at Grandma's" will be like each year—she chooses a different theme and makes all-new decorations, dinnerware, and package wraps to carry it out. Even the menu matches!

A Florida couple decks the halls with a tropical focus. A Houston family decorates in a savory Southwest style, while a fellow Texan frames her door with angels. In each case, the theme expresses personal interests and individuality.

The idea of using themes fired our imaginations this year, and we hope it will inspire you, too. May you enjoy your celebrations and all the preparations, and may your home be filled with the generous spirit of the season.

Christmas Around the South

A Gracious Welcome in Galveston

At the turn of the century, Galveston, Texas, claimed to be the "Wall Street of the Southwest." Financiers and entrepreneurs had built a center of business fortune on an island that was not much more than a sandbar, two miles off the coast in the Gulf of Mexico. Among these businessmen was William L. Moody, Jr., who had firmly established his family name in banking, insurance, hotels, newspapers, and cotton. William, his wife, Libbie, and their four children—Mary, William Lewis III, Shearn, and Libbie—enjoyed wealth and social position.

The city was known for its ever-changing business climate, but its residents also had to be prepared to adapt to sudden and dramatic changes in the weather. In 1900 a tremendous hurricane struck Galveston. While many people chose to leave the city following the devastation, the Moodys and other leading families chose to stay, fortifying the island and rebuilding the city.

It was at this time that William Moody purchased a stately home of red brick and limestone located at 2618 Broadway, a very fashionable Galveston address. The Moody Mansion, as it came to be known, was among the first houses in Texas to be constructed on a steel frame and to be equipped with electricity. While Libbie and the children vacationed at a family-owned resort in the Virginia mountains, William stayed in the city, finalizing the purchase of the house. He wrote often to his dear "Hib," as he called her. About the mansion, he wrote, "Well, Hib, we may live and die in a palace yet."

The Moodys usually celebrated Christmas quietly with just the family and close friends, but there were occasions when festive holiday parties were in order. The first was December 11, 1911, when,

at the age of 19, daughter Mary made her debut. The *Galveston Daily News* reported that the Moodys had hosted "a very smart gathering of fashionable people." Two hundred guests formally welcomed Mary into Texas society.

Four years later, in December 1915, Mary became the bride of E.C. Northen, a Galveston insurance executive. Again, the Moodys spared

Above: English-born architect William H. Tyndall designed the 31-room brick and limestone house with bay windows and bold, arcaded porches to catch the cooling breezes. His Romanesque design shows some affinities with the works of major architects of the day, notably Richard Morris Hunt and Henry Hobson Richardson. In the mansion cupola, Mary Moody Northen decorated a tree for the community each Christmas.

Opposite: The Christmas tree, decorated as Mary Moody Northen would have done, stands in the entrance hall. The magnificent stained glass window is inscribed with the motto, "Welcome Ever Smiles," from Shakespeare's Troilus & Cressida.

no expense to celebrate this event in the life of their eldest and favorite child.

At Christmas now, the newlyweds would open gifts at their own home before coming to the family mansion. Mary, in her correspondence with friends, described how she and her husband would exchange surprises on Christmas morning. Mary was quite inventive in packaging her gifts for him. One year she hung the clothing she had bought him on the wall, surrounded by colored lights and draped in silver tinsel. Another year, to package some equestrian tack, she created a horse head from paper bags and gave it a Spanish moss mane. Through the day, Mary and her husband would call on friends and relatives and then join her family for dinner at the Moody Mansion. On Christmas evening, the family visited the vaudeville or went to the moving pictures for entertainment.

The mansion on Broadway served not only as a home for the Moody family but also as the center for their financial empire and cotton companies. In the late 1930s, William Moody, Jr., turned to Mary to assume control of the family businesses. Nightly, he educated her in the intricacies of finance and corporate politics. When he died in 1954, Mary, herself recently widowed, stepped up to take control of the family interests and returned to live in the family home.

Christmas traditions at the Moody Mansion changed. Mary loved Christmas and all the trappings of the season. She was quite childlike in her

Above left: A hand-tinted photograph of Mary Elizabeth Moody, age 19, is found on the ornately carved Japanese desk in the library. Mary and her relatives wrote many letters and saved countless Christmas cards and notes.

Left: Quiet family holiday gatherings took place in the library. The Gorham sterling silver service on display here was a wedding gift to Libbie and William L. Moody, Jr., in 1890. The mantel arrangement includes milo (grain sorghum), sago palm, asparagus fern, cockscomb, and golden euonymus. Elegant French wired ribbon adorns the mirror sconces.

Below and left: The dining room features mahogany paneling, a plaster frieze gilded with Dutch metal, and a coffered ceiling. Above the fireplace, a bas-relief, painted to look like bronze, depicts a fox hunt. A topiary of pomegranates, wild lemons, freeze-dried roses, nuts, dyed boxwood cones, juniper, and French wired ribbon graces the Colonial Revival dining table.

7

Above: Preserved forever are the sentimental details of the Moodys' lives. In Mary's bedroom, archivists have re-created the December day of her debut. The Spanish silk-embroidered shawl belonged to Libbie Shearn Moody, Mary's mother. The opera glasses, holder, and velvet bag were gifts to the debutante from her mother.

celebration, choosing vivid colors and lacing traditional garlands with sparkling lights. Friends and companions surrounded the Texas heiress during the holidays. Mary was modest and quiet, but she liked to be in a festive setting in the company of her close friends.

In the 1950s, Mary added many decorations to enhance her celebration of the season. While she continued to have the family tree set up in the living room, she also decorated a grand tree in the entrance hall. A third tree, covered with twinkling lights, was placed outside, in the mansion's cupola, to delight all who might pass by.

In 1983, Galveston was again struck by a hurricane. Although the Moody Mansion remained structurally sound, water soaked the house's interior and flooded the electrical system. Fortunately, Mary was vacationing when the storm hit. When she returned, she stayed a few blocks from the mansion to oversee the repair. She would never live in the family home again.

Mary had a mind for business and a heart for history. As a businesswoman who actively supported her interest in American history, she contributed generously to many cultural and historical agencies. As the Moody Mansion renovation progressed, Mary, now in her early 90s, recognized the opportunity to have her family home preserved as a museum. She envisioned the Moody Mansion as a lens through which visitors might see a bygone era. Begun while Mary was alive, the refurbishing was continued after her death in 1986 by a private foundation she had established.

Today the Moody Mansion and Museum offers visitors a remarkable view of an upper-middle-class American home of the early 20th century. Carefully saved family letters and diaries, business documents, military records, political commentaries, and personal correspondence—literally tens of thousands of scraps of paper held dear by the Moody family—now comprise a priceless archive, representative of life at the turn of the century. The Moody Mansion, restored to its original splendor and decorated to celebrate the Christmas season, extends Mary Moody Northen's gracious invitation to the past.

8

THE MOODY CHRISTMAS CARD COLLECTION

Among the Moody family papers are almost 30,000 greeting cards, the most interesting of which are Christmas cards. Their design and style tell much about United States history and the hopes and concerns of the American people.

The oldest cards in the collection are dated 1909 and 1910. These were similar to traditional social calling cards. Designs were small and refined, often hand-painted in watercolor.

In the late 1920s, the United States was reveling in post-war prosperity. Christmas cards were larger, the colors more garish, and the designs, for the most part, secular. Also quite popular with these "modern" Americans were themes reminiscent of colonial times.

As American spirits declined during the Great Depression, so did the splendor of Christmas cards. The envelopes were no longer lined, and colors and pictures were greatly simplified. Religious messages announced the revival of faith for many people.

The 1940s and World War II brought newfound optimism. Cards again featured vivid colors, and patriotic themes appeared. In the 1950s, Americans focused on home and family. Christmas greetings, "from our house to yours," often arrived illustrated with pen-and-ink drawings of the sender's residence.

The Christmas card collection and other private letters are part of rotating displays at the Moody Mansion and Museum in Galveston.

Top right: From the formal 1900s through the frivolous 1920s to the patriotic 1940s, Christmas card designs have reflected the changing American spirit.

Center right: During the Great Depression, friends exchanged cards that were smaller and simpler than those of the 1920s.

Bottom right: Christmas cards from the 1920s featured lavish graphics and envelope liners in colors that "danced."

Melrose Spins a Fascinating Tale

At Melrose plantation, a few miles south of Natchitoches, Louisiana, Christmas is celebrated with simplicity. Red bows and greenery stand out crisply against the white railing of the upstairs gallery of the "big house." Grapevine wreaths hang at the downstairs windows. Inside, the dining room and parlor are decorated with fruit, greenery, and dried flowers, and the tree is hung with natural ornaments. The rustic decorations complement the building, which is a typical Louisiana plantation house. If the house is typical, however, its history is not.

Completed in 1833 by Jean Baptiste Louis Metoyer, it symbolizes the success of a large family whose founder, Marie Thérèze Coincoin, was a second-generation African slave. In the 20th century, it became a thriving cultural center that attracted dozens of Southern writers and artists and produced one of America's foremost primitive painters.

The story begins with Marie Thérèze. Born in Natchitoches in 1742, she was hired out in 1767 to a 23-year-old French merchant, Claude Thomas Pierre Metoyer. The two formed an

Opposite top: Grasses, berries, peppers, and a raffia bow dress up a simple vine wreath on each ground-floor window.

Opposite: Completed in 1833, the "big house" is the centerpiece of Melrose plantation. The octagonal wings were added early in the 20th century.

Above right: The Yucca House, built around 1796, was home to Marie Thérèze Coincoin. The framework of cypress timbers is filled in with bousillage, a mixture of mud, deer hair, and Spanish moss.

Right: Writer François Mignon called this two-story structure the African House, because it reminded him of huts in the Congo. Built about 1800 by Louis Metoyer, it is believed to have been a jail for slaves.

11

Above: To give a stylish twist to the wreath of holly, magnolia, and fern, florist Jackie Smith added chili peppers, apples, loops of ribbon attached to florist's picks, and calamondin oranges from her back yard. The peppers, holly, and oranges also add interest to the garland that swags the mantel.

alliance that was to last 20 years and produce seven sons and three daughters.

Metoyer eventually purchased and freed Marie Thérèze and all of their children and in 1786, he gave her a tract of 68 acres along the Cane River. In colonial Louisiana, with its predominantly French, Roman Catholic culture, free people of color enjoyed more economic freedom than did their counterparts in the United States. Hardworking and ambitious, Marie Thérèze and her children multiplied the 68 acres into more than 11,000, with nearly 100 slaves to help work the land. By the time of her death in 1816 or 1817, the family was one of the wealthiest in the area known as Isle Brevelle, a close-knit community that is still intact today.

Christmas decorations at Melrose do not reflect any historical period. They simply bring a holiday look to rooms that are furnished much as they were through most of this century, when John and Cammie Garrett Henry lived here. The Henrys inherited the plantation in 1898 from John's father. "Miss Cammie," devoted to the preservation and promotion of Louisiana history and culture, restored the houses and outbuildings and then welcomed artists and writers to come and pursue their creative projects. The long list of luminaries who accepted her invitation includes Erskine Caldwell, William Faulkner, Caroline Dormon, Lyle Saxon, Harnett Kane, Alexander Woollcott, and Alberta Kinsey.

Kinsey, a New Orleans artist, inadvertently helped produce homegrown talent at Melrose. In the 1940s, Clementine Hunter, longtime maid and cook at the plantation, found oil paints that the artist had left behind and tried her hand at "marking" a picture. Over the next 40 years she produced hundreds of paintings drawn from her memories of plantation life. Hunter was quickly recognized as a brilliant primitive painter, and her work was featured in museums and magazines nationwide. Today some of her murals are displayed in the African House and Yucca House.

In 1971, the Association for the Preservation of Historic Natchitoches acquired the plantation, which was declared a National Historic Landmark in 1974. Open for tours daily, Melrose offers a fascinating encounter with Louisiana's rich history and complex culture.

Above: When Cammie Garrett Henry was mistress of Melrose (1898-1948), the plantation became an artists' retreat. Artists and writers could stay as long as they liked, provided they were productive. Every evening those in residence would gather here at the dinner table and report on their day's work.

Top: A fan of peacock feathers, eucalyptus, and statice frames a rustic birdhouse to make an unusual and imaginative tree topper.

13

A Grand House
For the Governor

The weather is pleasantly warm for the Christmas open house at the North Carolina Executive Mansion in Raleigh. While a crowd on the steps waits patiently to see the lavishly decorated first-floor rooms, families pose for snapshots out on the broad front walk.

The open house is a popular event: Nearly a third of the 40,000 visitors who toured the governor's residence in 1991 came during this four-day period to see the elegant mansion dressed in Christmas finery. The decorations, assembled and hung by volunteers and the mansion staff, suit the

Above: The Queen Anne-style Executive Mansion in Raleigh, North Carolina, was designed by Philadelphia architect Samuel Sloan in 1883 and completed in 1891.

Left: The hand-hooked red and gold carpet in the entrance hall commemorates the Executive Mansion's centennial. The center medallion includes symbols of the state and its capital. Portraits of previous governors line the walls.

15

Above: The state flower, bird, and shell (Scotch bonnet) hang from the branches of this North Carolina-grown Fraser fir. Garlands of sweetgum balls strung on fishing line and sprayed gold alternate with paper-twist ribbon for a festive effect.

grandeur of the interiors, yet offer creative ideas that people can apply in their own homes.

According to social director Terry Chambliss, planning for Christmas begins in spring, when she meets with First Lady Dorothy Martin, floral artist Grady Wheeler, and longtime volunteer Dorothy Luck to discuss ideas. "We always use as many North Carolina products as possible," says Terry. Almost everything, including trees and greenery, is donated by individuals or businesses in the state.

In the gentlemen's parlor, a towering Fraser fir twinkles with 11,000 lights. The ornaments are state symbols (cardinals, silk and gold dogwood blossoms, gilded Scotch bonnets) and state resources or products—sand dollars from the coast, glass balls and bells made in Gastonia, and garlands of gilded sweetgum balls. Wheeler first created a North Carolina tree in this room in 1986,

A 14-foot-tall tree decorated with state symbols dominates the south drawing room or gentlemen's parlor. Over the mantel, garland wrapped with drapery cord (and hung with fishing line and eye hooks) frames the Rococo Revival mirror. Reproductions and antiques furnish the room. Green silk damask, a copy of 19th-century fabric, hangs at the windows and covers the sofa.

16

and Governor Martin liked it so much that he requested the same kind of tree every year for as long as he remained in office. "It's traditional now," says Grady. "People come looking for it."

The house's sophisticated interiors contrast sharply with the Victorian exterior. In 1883, when Governor Thomas J. Jarvis hired noted Philadelphia architect Samuel Sloan to design the building, the Queen Anne style was considered to be both eminently domestic and an up-to-date symbol of technological progress. (The characteristic "gingerbread" woodwork, for example, was made possible by the invention of steam-powered jigsaws and lathes.)

By 1925, however, Victorian architecture was old-fashioned, and the first-floor rooms were updated in the neoclassical style, giving them the more formal look they have today. In these rooms, the state's governors and their wives have held inaugural balls and state dinners, promoted political programs and charitable causes, entertained dignitaries and business groups, and welcomed busloads of tourists and school children.

Three times over the last 100 years there have been calls to abandon the structure. Each time the move was rejected in favor of renovation and preservation. In 1967, the Executive Mansion Fine Arts Committee (EMFAC) was established to oversee the protection and maintenance of the house. As the building's centennial approached, Dorothy Martin helped create the Executive Mansion Fund, Inc., an endowment that supports the work of EMFAC and provides for a curator, educational programs, and publications. The house was placed on the National Register of Historic Places in 1970. Today, its future secure, the Executive Mansion continues to serve admirably the purpose that Governor Jarvis envisioned, providing an appropriate setting for the governor "to dispense the hospitality incumbent upon him and due to the State."

Above: Arrangements of greenery, deer antlers, and tobacco "hands" (bundles of leaves tied with another leaf) hang on the wooden blinds that cover the tall windows in the library. Reproduction Chippendale chairs are pulled up to the leather-topped conference table, where Governor Martin holds budget and strategy meetings. The heart pine woodwork was stripped and stained in 1983.

Opposite: For the library overmantel, floral artist Grady Wheeler designed an enormous badge featuring elk antlers, Burford holly, white pine, and cotton. Below it are a French doré clock and matching candelabra.

Patrick Henry's Christmas

"Governor Henry, our Tidewater planters are very restless and nervous at the prospects of a possible British invasion of the capital," says Edmund Randolph. "Also, there is much talk of British war ships sailing up the James and the Potomac to bombard patriot homes."

The time is December 1776. The place is Scotchtown, the Virginia plantation home of Patrick Henry, who has just come home for the holidays. Randolph, Lieutenant Governor Page, and a delegation of worried citizens arrive to express their concern over defenses at Williamsburg. After the governor assures them that everything is under control, he invites everyone inside, where fiddle and harpsichord are playing and Henry's guests are dancing.

While the speaking parts in this production are taken by volunteers from the Patrick Henry-Scotchtown Committee, everyone who attends Scotchtown by Candlelight can get into the act. "We make it a real community event," says Ron Steele, committee chairman. Visitors gather at the end of the drive, most of them with lanterns or candles in hand, and play the role of Patrick Henry's neighbors. The actors representing the Williamsburg delegation join them in a procession to Henry's back door, where the play takes place.

Inside the house, dancers from Colonial Williamsburg perform reels and minuets, and

Above left: Edmund Randolph (left) and Lieutenant Governor John Page (in blue) present their concerns about a possible British invasion to a patient-looking Patrick Henry (in green).

Left: Mr. Reynolds, Patrick Henry's overseer, waxes enthusiastic about a bowl he made for the governor. He'd like to present it to him and request a few days' leave, but Mrs. Syme is unmoved. "Mr. Reynolds, the governor is entertaining an important guest for the holidays. Can this not wait until a more convenient time?"

Above: A bust of Patrick Henry stands in the entrance hall of Scotchtown, Henry's home from 1771 until 1777. The property's name reflects an earlier owner's hope that a Scottish settlement would develop on the surrounding land.

Left: A pyramid of oranges and boxwood is a colorful variation on the apple pyramids of Colonial Williamsburg. Using the oranges to hold votive candles is an inventive 20th-century touch.

volunteers from the Scotchtown Committee enact vignettes depicting typical colonial social activities.

Visitors can tour the home at their own pace, and there are costumed guides in each room to answer any questions they might have. This is the only time during the year that the house can be seen by candlelight. The effect is spectacular, says Steele. "We try to make the way the house looks as factual as possible," he says. "It's a real history lesson, especially for the children." After the candlelight tour, visitors are invited to the detached kitchen for ginger cookies and cider.

Scotchtown was Patrick Henry's home during the most critical and active years of his political life. He bought the large house and 1,000 acres in 1771 and brought his wife and their six children here. It was at Scotchtown that he wrote his famous "liberty or death" speech, which he delivered in Richmond with such high drama and power that one eyewitness said it "electrified the assembly."

On June 29, 1776, Henry was elected the first governor of Virginia. Less than a week later, the Declaration of Independence was signed, and the American Revolution began. When he was reelected in 1777, Henry moved to Williamsburg and sold Scotchtown the following year.

Located near Richmond, not far from I-95, Scotchtown is normally open daily from April through October. It reopens on the first weekend in December especially for this event. For a modest admission fee, you can get into the holiday spirit, 18th-century style, and experience a bit of American history in a lively and imaginative way.

Above left: Sergeant Clark, General Greene, and Lieutenant Randall play a card game called loo in the gentlemen's drawing room. The actors are all volunteers from the Patrick Henry-Scotchtown Committee.

Left: Patrick Henry's writing table with extension arms, probably designed to support maps, was made in England or Virginia about 1760. Henry's father was a mapmaker. A reproduction of his work hangs on the wall.

The Reindeer Are Racing in Houston

It's a chilly, overcast day in Houston, but that doesn't stop thousands of runners of all ages from turning out for the annual AppleTree Jingle Bell Run. For the last nine years, this race has promoted family fun with a witty Yuletide emphasis. Participants are encouraged to come dressed for the holidays—and they do, decked out as Christmas trees, packages, reindeer, Santa Clauses, even a star followed by "Wise Persons."

It's the biggest race in Houston now, with 8,500 runners last year, and in the spirit of the season, it's all for a good cause. Funds raised go to support the Youth and Urban Services Department of the Downtown YMCA. The department offers summer day camps, overnight camping, after-school child care, a food bank, Meals on Wheels, and programs for seniors.

With four races during the morning, there's something for everyone. The Kids' Run follows a one-mile course. The Big Bell (for serious runners) and Wheelchair races are five miles, and the Family Walk is three miles. Awards go to the top 20 male, female, and children's finalists and the top five wheelchair finalists. The best costumes also win awards, and there's a special category for Centipede Runners—teams that run the entire course together. Last year, one team dressed as a Christmas train, and another, representing Houston Light and Power Company, ran as the meter, the meter reader, and a dog.

Top right: Volunteer race monitors hold back eager participants in the Kids' Run, one of four races in Houston's AppleTree Jingle Bell Run.

Center right: Mr. and Mrs. Santa Claus lead off the Kids' Run in a sled pulled by a truck.

Bottom right: Running (or walking) is a family activity in this annual event, whose proceeds support the Youth and Urban Services Department of the Downtown YMCA.

23

It's the costumes that make this race fun, and some participants seem not to mind sacrificing speed to creativity. Others just pull on the specially designed T-shirt that all registrants receive, add a pair of sponge or paper antlers, and voilà, a racing reindeer is born.

AppleTree, a food store chain, has been the primary corporate sponsor for the past several years, with additional support provided by a local radio station. At the end of the race, exhausted participants can renew their energy with fruit, snacks, and punch provided by AppleTree, or they can indulge in a piece of the four-foot-long cake from the store's bakery.

The Jingle Bell Run is an ingenious way to celebrate the season—it's a race that everybody wins. The food store gets publicity, the YMCA raises money, and the runners have a really good time.

Above: Santa and his reindeer wear the T-shirts that participants receive when they register.

Center left: Runners get into the holiday spirit with creative costumes like this paper Christmas tree edged with garland.

Bottom left: The "cars" in this Christmas train ran the whole race together, in a category called Centipede Runners.

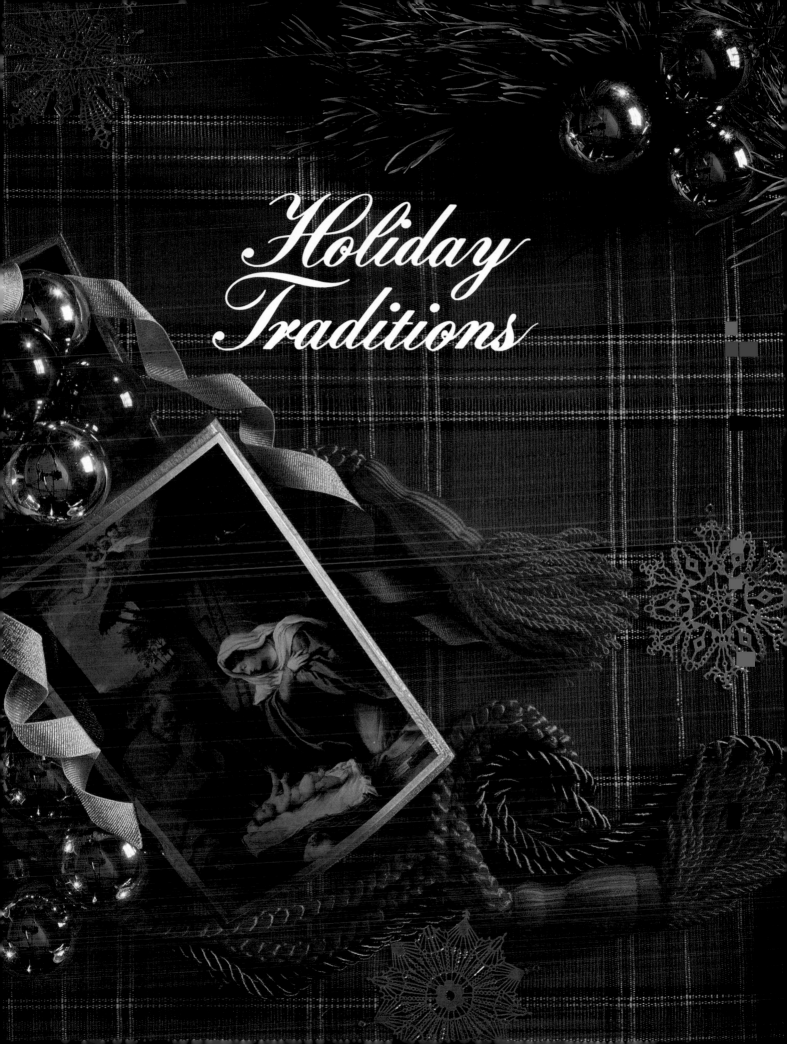

Holiday Traditions

Holiday Variety Is The Spice of Her Life

Above: Georgie painted the china with her own design of waving wheat and fired it in her kiln. To make the topiaries, she tied bunches of wheat with raffia and secured them in clay pots with florist's clay. Sphagnum moss packed into the pot helps hold the wheat upright. A bookplate serves as a name card.

"Everybody had a white damask tablecloth to use for Sundays," says Georgie. This one was her mother's. The butter dish and salt dips are antiques from her late husband's family.

If variety is the spice of life, then Georgie Hederhorst's Christmases are very spicy indeed. Every year, this Baytown, Texas, grandmother devises a new theme for her family's celebration—and then she creates decorations, ornaments, gift wraps, quilts, table linens, even dinnerware and costumes to carry it out.

Last year, she drew on memories of her childhood in Bucklin, Kansas, to create "Christmas on a Kansas Wheat Farm." It gave her a chance to share family history with her children and grandchildren, who could scarcely imagine life without electricity, much less Christmas without an evergreen tree. But, says Georgie, "where I lived in western Kansas, there were no trees, except cottonwoods and willows and fruit trees around the farmers' houses. So we'd cut a big branch and wrap it in green tissue paper. And we always made

Above: Georgie Hederhorst of Baytown, Texas, decorates her house with a different theme every Christmas. Last year, she re-created the kind of tree she had as a child on a Kansas wheat farm.

27

all our Christmas decorations, because that was the fun of it, making our own." Paper chains and paper dolls, yarn dolls, and strings of popcorn and peanuts in the shell hung from the branches last year as they did in her childhood. "We'd also hang spools of thread for bright color," she says. "Some of our neighbors used candles, but my father would never let us have them because of the danger of fire."

The theme also gave Georgie's grandchildren—and some of her Texas friends—their first look at wheat. "I was surprised at how many of my friends, some of them 75 years old, had never seen wheat!" she says. Appropriately, the grain provided the key motif for decorations: Using wheat from the family farm, which Georgie still owns, she fashioned topiaries, napkin rings, and wreaths. Wheat also inspired the design for one of three sets of china that she painted for use on Christmas Day. On each chair at the dining table, she hung a burlap stocking, tied with upholstery braid and decorated with an ornament, branches, and beads. "The switches were just for the fun of it," she says.

Georgie has been doing theme Christmases ever since she and her late husband, Fred, were first married. Past motifs have included birds, music, the garden, cowboys, cookies, Hawaii, and Japan. Everybody's favorite part seems to be dinner, and not just because of the meal. When they come to the table, the family dons the costumes that Georgie has made. Last year it was straw hats and bandannas for the men and aprons and bonnets for the women. "We have fun dressing up," says Georgie. "It makes for conversation—and a lot of laughter." Her daughter-in-law, Brenda, says,"One of my favorite themes was 'Crystal and Lace.' The women wore lace gloves and the men wore lace garters, and there was crystal everywhere."

All of the china, decorations, and costumes from nearly 50 years' worth of Christmases are stored in Georgie's attic. "My children won't let me get rid of it," she says. "They borrow it when they have parties."

These theme Christmases involve a tremendous amount of work, but, says Georgie, "as long as you have fun, you don't care." And as Brenda notes, "The best part is that we have some *wonderful* memories."

Above: Each person's chair is decorated with a stocking. Everyone dresses for dinner here—Georgie provides the theme-related costume. Last year it was straw hats and bandannas for the men, aprons and bonnets for the women.

To carry out her Kansas theme, Georgie turned a ring of barbed wire into a wreath and embellished it with red ribbon, wheat, and a horseshoe.

MERRY
CHRISTMAS

Above: There are more than 30 varieties of cookies to choose from at the annual Cookie Push. Ready to fill their baskets are Mary Myers, Gail Eggeman, Trudy Little, and India Woolums. This year's container is a basket with plaid ribbon woven around the middle. A small bow and jumbo jingle bells are secured to the front, and a sheet of red cellophane serves as a liner.

Cookies and Friends: The More, the Merrier

The hustle and bustle that accompanies the month of December rarely leaves time for baking more than a batch or two of your family's favorite holiday cookies. Yet Gail Eggeman and Mary Myers of St. Petersburg, Florida, have plenty of homemade goodies, sometimes up to 30 assorted varieties. And they only spend an hour or so in the kitchen. "I love Christmas and I've always loved to bake, but you can only make so many different treats yourself," Gail explains, "so Mary and I decided it would be fun to get together with a lot of friends and have a big cookie swap."

Now into its seventh year, the Cookie Push is held on Sunday afternoon two weeks before Christmas. (That way husbands are usually at home, so there's no need for babysitters.) About 30 guests attend, each armed with a batch of mouth-watering cookies.

"Our friends really enjoy coming to the party to chat with people they haven't seen in a year, but the husbands and kids love it because the women bring so many different kinds of cookies home!" says Gail.

Sources for the sweets range from old family favorites to the newest recipes in holiday magazines. But regardless of how delicious a guest's cookies may be, Gail and Mary find that guests still often arrive with tales about what went wrong in the kitchen. "We call it 'cookie insecurity'," says Gail.

The cookies are off-limits until each basket is filled, but tasty hors d'oeuvres and bite-size tidbits are served, along with "Cookie Push Punch."

Gail and Mary take turns hosting the party. Preparations begin weeks ahead of time, when they get together to make the invitations, cookie containers, and name tags for the containers. They also make recipe cards to accompany each invitation, so that the recipes can be compiled into a booklet that each guest receives after the holidays. The pair usually devises a theme for all of these elements. In the past, they've used red doilies centered on a snowy background, rubber-stamped Christmas trees and holly leaves with berries, and paper-punched motifs.

Last year, gingerbread men provided the theme. Gail and Mary made the invitation by tracing around a cookie cutter, enlarging the pattern on a copy machine, and then outlining the design with dimensional paint. To decorate the homemade envelopes and recipe cards, they made a rubber stamp by carving a gingerbread man out of a small eraser. For the recipe booklet, they cut the motif from a sponge and sponge-painted the cover, adding hole-punched hearts below the date.

"Containers for the cookies are probably the hardest part of the planning, because it's so hard to find 35 or 40 of the same thing," Gail confesses. "Baskets have worked the best, although we have also decorated tins and cardboard Shaker boxes."

After the holidays are over, Gail and Mary compile the guests' cookie recipes, along with the recipes for the party fare. They admit that the booklet is sometimes mailed as late as July or August, because producing it takes a little longer than it should ("after Christmas is Valentine's Day, and after Valentine's Day, Easter . . ."). But better late than never. Besides, it reminds friends that the next Christmas Cookie Push is just around the corner!

If you want to organize your own Cookie Push, Gail and Mary offer the following tips:

❧ Include a recipe card with the invitation or ask everyone to bring their own to the party so that compiling the "Cookie Push Recipe Booklet" will be fairly easy.

❧ Line the cookie container with grease-proof paper, such as cellophane, wax paper, or foil.

❧ To make it easier for guests to carry home their cookie-filled containers, place the containers in paper bags and label each with a name tag.

Above: Gail and Mary used a gingerbread motif for the invitation, recipe card, envelope, and recipe booklet last year. They made the invitation by tracing around a cookie cutter, enlarging the pattern, and then outlining the design with dimensional paint.

Top: Guests gather around Gail's kitchen island to enjoy hors d'oeuvres, punch, and each other's company. Later, after all the cookie baskets have been filled, they can sample the sweets.

31

Two Hundred Thousand Ornaments, And Still Counting!

Clara Johnson Scroggins of Tampa, Florida, could decorate 4,000 trees with her collection of ornaments—she has 200,000 of them and adds more every year. The author of six books (*Silver Christmas Ornaments: A Collector's Guide* and five editions of *Hallmark Keepsake Ornaments: A Collector's Guide*), Scroggins is probably the world's foremost authority on contemporary ornaments and is definitely one of the top collectors.

Her interest in the field began in December 1972, when she bought a sterling silver cross in memory of her husband, who had recently died. Later, she discovered that the ornament was a second edition, and she decided that she wanted the first. One telephone call led to another, and before long, Clara was immersed in the world of contemporary Christmas collectibles.

At that time, most ornaments were sold in sets of six or 12 and depicted traditional scenes. Today, says Clara, modern ornaments may be sold singly or in sets and they chronicle our times. "There are ornaments commemorating Desert Storm, the Star Trek series, and the fall of the Berlin Wall," she notes. Others champion a cause—to save the earth, save the children, or save endangered species. "Many even show the evolution of modern thinking," continues

Above left: Contemporary ornament collector Clara Johnson Scroggins holds "The Jeweled Bell of Christmas" from The House of Fabergé. It's one of only 200 made, crafted of sterling silver covered in gold and embellished with precious gems and pearls.

Left: Any collectible ornament can increase in value over time, says Clara. These porcelain and gold ornaments from the Franklin Mint were inspired by Wedgwood jasperware and illustrate various Christmas carols.

Clara. "Santa doesn't smoke a pipe anymore, and he may be depicted as an avid skier, a hiker, or a jogger. Now if they'll just update Mrs. Claus!"

Clara says that anyone interested in joining the 80 million collectors of contemporary ornaments should remember the following:

🐾 If possible, buy the first edition in a series. Limited Edition and Collectible Series sell fast, so buy them early in the season.

🐾 Keep all original packaging and anything that comes with the ornament. This provides proof of purchase and age, and the box is specifically designed to protect the ornament.

🐾 Store ornaments in a cool, dry place. Heat and humidity cause metals to rust or corrode and fabrics to rot and fade. The glue used in the new injection-molded ornaments will also disintegrate under such conditions. Bread dough ornaments should be kept in airtight containers so that mice won't be attracted to them.

Clara keeps most of her collection in storage until Christmas, but during the year, she lends selected pieces to museums and festivals around the country. Eventually, she plans to donate most of her collection to a museum, although some of the ornaments will go to her family.

With so many different kinds of ornaments available, what types have yet to be created? "We have ornaments that have light, sounds, voices, and motion," says Clara. "I expect that one day I'll have an ornament that will put the tree up, hang itself on the tree, wrap the packages, and cook Christmas dinner!"

Above right: The Starship Enterprise ornament, commemorating the 25th anniversary of "Star Trek," sold out as soon as it was released and quintupled in value by the end of the year. Clara devised her own way to store Hallmark's "Oreo" and "Cherry Jubilee" ornaments.

Right: On a vine wreath painted white, Clara displays ornaments that honor family relationships. Contemporary decorations like these from Hallmark are collectible because designs are produced in limited numbers for one year only.

Right: Hallmark has issued a new hinged-walnut ornament every year since 1987. Shown here are "Nutshell Nativity" and "Nutshell Chat."

A Party with a Purpose

Marbury and Kathy Rainer believe that you can do something worthwhile and still have a good time. So when the Rainers invite friends to their family Christmas party, they ask them to bring new toys or other Christmas gifts to fill Santa's sleigh for Atlanta's homeless.

This year, the family decided to celebrate an old-fashioned Christmas. The Rainers and their sons (Justin, 10, and Evans, 6) dressed in Victorian costumes and looked as if they had just stepped out of a Currier & Ives lithograph. Even Santa's sleigh was an antique that Kathy had bought and placed on the back lawn especially for the occasion.

For decorations inside the house, Kathy created mouth-watering tablescapes with confections from her favorite bakeries. Teddy bear cookies and snowman cupcakes were almost too cute to

Above: Santa Claus hugs a little guest to thank her for the toy she put in his sleigh. The Rainers' friends brought nearly 200 presents, which a missionary from their church distributed to needy families in the inner city.

The Rainers issue 250 invitations to their family Christmas party. Here guests are inspired to join in a carol sing-along in the Rainers' living room. Throughout the house, everyone finds lively entertainment.

Above: Marbury and Kathy Rainer and their sons, Justin and Evans, enjoy a nostalgic carriage ride past their Buckhead home just before their holiday party begins. The family, dressed in Victorian costume, welcomes guests to an old-fashioned Christmas.

eat. Villages of gingerbread houses and gumdrop trees, made by Kathy and her niece, decorated the dining room table. Her sons' toy locomotive carried a cargo of hard candy and soft peppermint sticks. In the library, Kathy opened Santa's Candy Store where a friend, costumed as an elf, filled the children's orders. Little guests carried home gumdrops, lollipops, chocolates, gumballs, and gummy bears in white paper bags. Kathy laughs that one little boy told her it was the best party he had ever been to because he could eat all the cookies and candy he wanted!

Also for the children, a workshop was set up where they could make candy cane reindeer with chenille-wire antlers, red pom-pom noses, and jiggly eyes.

Enjoying Atlanta's mild December weather, guests flowed in and out of the Rainers' home, finding entertainment wherever they paused. A barber shop quartet sang old-fashioned carols. Horse-drawn carriages, hired for the party, made tours through the Buckhead neighborhood. On the front lawn, Justin and the older boys played a rousing game of football, while Evans and his friends found thrills on a homemade roller coaster in the backyard.

Santa Claus circulated among the Rainers' friends. When one wide-eyed little girl asked him what was in his sack, Santa replied, "What's in my bag? Well, today my sack is empty because today is the day *you* bring toys to give to the needy." The child smiled and pointed to the toys, blankets, and clothes overflowing from the sleigh on the Rainers' lawn. Santa smiled, too.

Above left: An antique tricycle and a toy locomotive bring a touch of whimsy to one of Kathy's table displays. To create height and add interest, Kathy first arranges boxes of varying sizes on the tabletop. She then drapes yards of gold lamé over the boxes to make a festive setting for trays of cookies and cakes.

Left: Santa's Candy Store opens for business in the library. Books have been moved out and sugarplums brought in, making dreams come true for junior partygoers.

The Sweetest Lady In Town

Of all the late-night visits Santa must make on Christmas Eve, Elizabeth Chanslor's house is probably one of his favorite stops. Nowhere else is he likely to find a more scrumptious treat than Elizabeth's Creamy Pulled Candy. And he's not the only sweet tooth she's hooked!

Requests pour in from all over Bourbon County, Kentucky, for this creamy confection, keeping her busy for a good part of the year, but especially at Christmastime. Made by combining sugar and cream, then pulling until the mixture turns white and has an elastic texture, the candy must be cut into bite-size pieces with kitchen shears before it hardens. "I'd be out of business if my scissors ever broke!" Elizabeth exclaims. Making the candy is strictly a fair-weather activity, she adds. On rainy days, the candy won't hold its shape as well.

This family tradition began with Elizabeth's husband's stepmother, Sue Chanslor. "She would fill a big tin can full of the candy and give it to my husband, Ronald, as a gift. It was his very favorite Christmas present," Elizabeth says.

Now into her 37th year as an expert candy-puller, Elizabeth says her biggest fan is still her husband. "There's a lot to be said for getting to a man's heart through his stomach," she chuckles. "Ronald married me for my jam cake, but it's my creamy pulled candy that's kept him!"

Above: Grandma is always Jonathan's favorite person, especially when it's time to make Creamy Pulled Candy.

ELIZABETH'S CREAMY PULLED CANDY

- 4 cups fine granulated sugar
  pinch of salt
- 1 cup boiling water
- 1 cup whipping cream
- 1 teaspoon vanilla extract

Combine first 3 ingredients in a large heavy saucepan; bring to a boil. Cover and cook, without stirring, over high heat 3 to 5 minutes. Uncover and slowly add whipping cream, keeping mixture boiling; do not stir. Reduce heat, and continue cooking until mixture reaches hard ball stage (260°). Remove from heat, and immediately pour syrup onto a buttered marble slab. (Do not scrape mixture from sides of pan.)

Sprinkle vanilla over surface of hot syrup; let stand 3 minutes or until edges begin to set. Begin scraping syrup with a metal spatula into a central mass; continue scraping and folding until vanilla is blended.

Pull mixture with fingertips, allowing a spread of about 15 inches between hands; then fold mixture in half. Repeat pulling and folding until consistency changes from sticky to elastic. Begin twisting while folding and pulling. Continue pulling until ridges on twists begin to hold their shape, about 5 to 10 minutes.

Pull candy into a long rope; using kitchen shears, cut rope into 1- to 1½-inch segments. Place candy on wax paper, and cover with a towel. Let stand overnight or until candy becomes creamy. Store in an airtight container. Yield: about 2 pounds.

Note: Do not double recipe. If more candy is needed, make 2 batches.

Old-World Santas Carry Trinkets And Treasures

Barbara Kelly has long been fascinated by the stories and traditions surrounding St. Nicholas, and for a time she collected new handmade Santas. But she was never convinced that the dolls other craftsmen offered were images of the European legend she loved. When the children's hospital sought donations for Atlanta's Festival of Trees, she decided to make and contribute a Santa Claus doll of her own design. "I didn't want the sparkling and the new," Barbara said. "I wanted to make a Santa from the Old World."

Barbara, however, was an open-heart surgical nurse, not a doll maker. A trip to the craft store soon changed that. From clay, she sculpted Santa's face, hands, and boots. While these baked in the kitchen oven, she stitched a soft 18-inch doll body. At the flea market, she bought old fur coats of coyote, red fox, and bear and from these she tailored St. Nicholas's robes.

To further the old-fashioned look, Barbara went antiques shopping for gifts to fill Santa's pack. He would carry not just one or two toys, but a sackful because, Barbara says, "That's how I want Santa to come to me, loaded down with things!"

Many of the treasures she selected were collectibles in themselves—vintage wooden tops, bisque dolls, and small chalkware rabbits, as well as brass ornaments and jingle bells made in the 1950s. She filled Santa's bag with so many marvelous trinkets that even she was overwhelmed by the detail.

To her delight, the three dolls she crafted brought high bids in the charity auction. Barbara has since limited her hours at the hospital to nurture her growing business, Snowbird Creations. At home, in Duluth, Georgia, her husband has even given over his once-orderly library to her busy workshop.

"My Santas are all cluttered—just the way my mind is, chaos," says Barbara. And from this creative chaos come her St. Nicholas dolls, capturing the abundant generosity of the old saint himself.

Above: His satchel filled with bayberry, a nutcracker, and many other trinkets, Barbara's Story Teller, trimmed in bear and red fox fur, pauses to share a Christmas tale. Barbara travels to Cape Cod each September to collect the bayberry used in her designs.

Top: Barbara Kelly loves St. Nicholas and the stories that have been told about him. She says she keeps one Santa in her house year-round because "it's good luck to keep Santa in the house."

Above: The Stable Keeper braves a Christmas blizzard to bring nuts and berries to the animals of the field. Barbara says, "I wanted my Santa to look real enough to walk through the blustery snow."

Above: Barbara loads treasures from yesterday into St. Nicholas's bag. On Christmas Eve, the Night Voyager travels by rocking horse, rewarding good children with antique toys and gifts such as miniature skates, drumsticks, and pocket watches.

The Chrismon Tradition

In a tradition that is rich in the symbols of Christmas, the congregation of Holmes Street United Methodist Church in Huntsville, Alabama, begins each Advent season by decorating a Chrismon tree. After sharing a potluck supper, the members participate in a special worship service in which the meanings of the Chrismons are explained through Bible readings and the singing of Christmas carols.

A Chrismon, a combination of the words *Christ* and *monogram,* is an ornament bearing a Christian symbol. Some of the symbols are based on images mentioned in the Bible and were first used in biblical times. The ornaments on the tree in the photograph at left include a crown, which signifies that Jesus is the ruler of all creation, and a chalice, a symbol for Communion. Strings of white lights are used on the tree to celebrate Jesus as the light of the world. The colors of Chrismons are symbolic also—white for the purity and gold for the majesty of Jesus.

The first Chrismon tree was used in the Lutheran Church of the Ascension in Danville, Virginia, in 1957. Since then, the Lutheran Church has helped spread this custom to churches all over the world by publishing instruction booklets for Chrismons like the ones on the tree at Holmes Street Church. Those ornaments are made with craft foam, beads, and other trims. On this page and the next, we offer instructions for cross-stitched and crocheted Chrismons, so that you can add the symbolism of these ornaments to your holiday traditions. (For more information on Chrismons and how to make them, check with a church library or church-affiliated bookstore.)

Inset opposite: During the latter part of the service, the children of the church come forward to choose a Chrismon and hang it on the tree.

Opposite: The Chrismon tree is a celebration of Jesus. Many of the ornaments are symbols for events that occurred during his life and ministry.

CROSS-STITCHED CHRISMONS

Materials (for 1 ornament):
charts on pages 154-55
5" square (14-count) white Aida cloth
DMC floss #743 Gold
3" square of fusible craft fleece
3½" square of gold fabric
4½" (⅛"-wide) gold ribbon

Center design on Aida cloth and work according to chart, using 3 strands of floss. Centering cross-stitch design, trim Aida cloth to 3½" square.

Following manufacturer's instructions, fuse craft fleece to wrong side of gold fabric. To make hanger, fold ribbon in half. With raw edges aligned, baste ribbon ends to top center on right side of cross-stitch piece. With right sides facing, raw edges aligned, and loop to inside, stitch cross-stitch piece to gold fabric with a ¼" seam, leaving an opening in bottom edge. Clip corners, turn, and slipstitch opening closed. Press.

CROCHETED CHRISMONS

Materials (for 1 ornament):
charts on pages 154-55
size 20 crochet cotton
size 8 steel crochet hook
scrap of gold fabric
scrap of fusible craft fleece
12½" (⅛"-wide) gold ribbon

With crochet cotton and size 8 hook, crochet design according to chart. Begin with a ch as specified on chart and dc in 6th ch from hook. * Ch 1, sk 1 ch, dc in next st, rep from * across, ch 4 and turn. To work an open square over an open square, dc in dc, ch 1, sk ch-1 sp, dc in dc. To work an open square over a filled square, dc in dc, ch 1, sk 1 dc, dc in next dc. To work a filled square over an open square, dc in dc, dc in ch-1 sp, dc in dc. To work a filled square over a filled square, dc in each dc. Lightly block finished crochet piece. From gold fabric, cut 2 pieces, ¼"

larger on all sides than blocked crochet piece. From craft fleece, cut 1 piece the same size as crochet piece. Following manufacturer's instructions, center and fuse craft fleece to wrong side of 1 gold piece. To make hanger, fold ribbon in half. With ribbon fold aligned with raw edge of fabric, baste ribbon to top center on right side of 1 gold piece. With right sides facing, raw edges aligned, and ribbon to inside, stitch gold fabric pieces together with a ¼" seam, leaving an opening in bottom edge. Clip corners, turn, and slipstitch opening closed. Press. Slipstitch edges of crochet piece to gold fabric ornament along seam.

Crochet Abbreviations:
ch—chain
dc—double crochet
rep—repeat
sk—skip
sp—space
st—stitch

Decorating for the Holidays

Season's Greetings
Start at the Door

Decorating for Christmas begins at the door, where the wreaths, garlands, and bows you hang extend a warm welcome to guests and a special greeting to all who pass by. Let your decorations express your own personality—here are three ideas to spark your creativity.

The symmetrical badge of pineapples, apples, and nandina berries at left is constructed on an Oasis-filled plastic cage (see page 49). Because the pineapples make the arrangement heavy, the cage is hung on the door first. That way, you can make sure the fruits are balanced properly.

Two long florist's stakes anchor each pineapple, and wire wrapped around the base of the leaves secures the fruits to each other. Leyland cypress serves as the background for boxwood, apples, and nandina berries. The outside row of apples is inserted in a U-shape that mirrors the arch of the pineapples. The apples' stem ends are angled so that they lead the eye across and around the arrangement.

Top right: Vines woven in a large oval shape provide the foundation for evergreens, bayberry, fruit, and dried materials. These are attached with florist's picks, hot glue, or simply woven into the vines. Sunflower heads make eye-catching focal points.

Right: Layering velvet bows and ribbons over raffia streamers underscores the mix of formal and rustic materials in the arrangement itself. Sunflower seedheads are sold as birdfeed, so you may have chickadees, cardinals, and titmice visiting your decorations.

Opposite: A trio of pineapples crowns this traditional badge. To determine the dimensions, use the distance from the top of the pineapple to the center of the foundation (here, an Oasis cage) as a guide for how long the background branches should be.

Above: Houston artist Gloria Becker Rasmussen tweaks convention with this wreath, which she embellished with silk flowers and dusted with gold spray paint before adding a variety of ribbons and tassels.

Combining traditional fruit and greenery with unusual dried materials achieves a sophisticated yet inviting look on the door and porch pictured on the previous page. Instead of wreaths, there are ovals of woven honeysuckle vine filling the door panels. Floral designer Lynn Mann wove the shapes on a wire form while the vine was fresh and let them dry in place. The resulting braid is dense enough so that she could simply work in stems of holly, cypress, pine, fir, bayberry, and magnolia. A large sunflower seedhead provides the focal point at the bottom. (These may be ordered through florists or found at farmers' markets.) Hot glue holds the okra pods and oakleaf hydrangea in place, and Lynn used florist's picks to secure the radishes and apples. For the bouquet on the porch, she wired a block of craft foam to the railing and then built the arrangement from the bottom up.

Over much of the South, December is too warm and humid for decorations of fresh fruit and greenery to be practical. The solution for many people is artificial garland. Houston artist Gloria Becker Rasmussen takes "permanent" materials a step further to create an elaborate entry with an angelic theme. Lining the arch at right is artificial garland wrapped with white lights and embellished with papier-mâché and terra-cotta cherubs, Mexican painted-tin angels, inexpensive silk flowers dusted with gold spray paint, and weatherproof metallic ribbon.

Silk flowers also decorate the wreath. With the flowers in place, Gloria sprayed the whole wreath lightly with gold to tone down the different colors. To add a lively sense of movement, she knotted and furled several kinds of wired ribbon around the wreath. By crumpling the ribbon and tucking it well into the branches instead of simply wrapping the shape, Gloria created a dense mosaic of contrasting textures and sparkling color. The result makes a wonderfully sumptuous welcome.

Opposite: Garden statuary and an overdoor plaque are as much a part of this entry's decorations as the angel-studded garland and beribboned wreath.

Above: Floral artist Grady Wheeler uses a florist's cage to construct traditional fruit-and-greenery door decorations. They are available from florists and florist supply shops, as well as some craft stores.

How to Make a Beautiful Badge

Grady Wheeler has been volunteering his services to help decorate the Executive Mansion in Raleigh, North Carolina, for the last six years (see pages 14-19). One of his favorite tools is an Oasis-filled florist's cage, which can make quick work of arrangements that hang on a wall or door. (The decorations on pages 18, 19, and 44 were made using these.) The cage extends the life of arrangements, because the Oasis holds water. Soak it thoroughly before beginning the arrangement and let it drain well before hanging. During the season, check the Oasis, and when it begins to dry, take the arrangement down, soak the foundation, and let it drain well before hanging the arrangement up again.

On these pages, Grady demonstrates how to assemble a badge for your door. He also offers these tips for success:

❦ Use several types of greenery. The more textures you have, the more interesting the arrangement will be.

❦ Use variegated foliage such as aucuba to provide highlights and relieve the heavy look of an all-green decoration.

❦ Insert the background material so that it curves away from you. That way, when you hang the arrangement, it will appear to hug the wall or the door. Any flat or fluffy material makes a good background—Leyland cypress was used here, but pine, juniper, and fir will also work.

❦ To preserve fruit in arrangements, dip or spray with clear floor wax after inserting florist's stakes and wires. If birds or squirrels are likely to visit your outdoor arrangement, however, it is kinder to omit this step.

❦ Instead of apples, try lemons, limes, and oranges; or for a more formal look, spray the fruit silver or gold. (But again, remember the birds.)

❦ When you use cuttings of berry-laden Burford holly, remove the leaves. They don't last as long as the berries, and removing them gives the berries more impact.

48

1. Start by outlining the shape with branches inserted at the back of the cage. Work evenly all the way around the cage to fill out the background.

2. Next insert whorls of magnolia leaves into the sides and top of the cage. This creates the body of the arrangement.

3. Fill in around the magnolia with stems of boxwood and variegated foliage. Remember to follow the main lines already established by the background material and the magnolia.

4. To attach fruit, insert a 15-inch-long florist's stake into the bottom. Cut a length of #21 florist's wire in half and push each half through the fruit near the bottom, at right angles.

5. Twist the wires down around the stake, keeping the wire as close as possible to the fruit. Cut the stake to the desired length, making an angled cut so that it can be pushed into the Oasis easily. Insert the fruit at the center and just above and below center to create a focal point.

6. Insert stems of Burford holly berries at an upward angle and toward the back of the arrangement to add line and color. Also insert some shorter stems at the front, to bring the design forward and give it depth.

7. Cinnamon sticks "spice it up," puns Grady. Like the berries, they should go in at different angles. To make them easier to insert, wire and tape them to florist's picks.

8. To add pinecones, Grady drills a hole in the bottom of the cone and secures a pick with hot glue. You could also wrap wire around the lowest layer of scales and wire the pinecone to a florist's pick.

*Above: After a trip to Tahiti,
Wayne and Vicki Dewey began
giving Christmas a tropical twist.*

*The "under the sea" tree fills one
corner of the living room. On the dining table, the theme continues with
shell-motif china, a porcelain
clamshell, and electric marine colors.*

Christmas
"Under the Sea"

A printed turquoise tablecloth, cobalt blue and aqua candles, and a brilliant purple lamé tree skirt are far from the traditional red-and-green color scheme that most people use at Christmastime. But for Wayne and Vicki Dewey of Tampa, Florida, it seemed natural to blend their love for the tropics with decorations for the holidays.

Above: Wide purple satin ribbon winds around the tree, and colorful, hand-carved fish dangle from the branches. Ornaments such as the Santa riding a dolphin and the pelican with its catch of the day focus on the couple's love of the beach.

51

Above: On a buffet in the dining room, Vicki assembled a tropical tablescape: a tabletop Christmas tree, a chunk of coral, a cement fish sculpture, and flowers from the garden. To pull the elements together, she painted the canvas above. The tabletop tree is a craft foam cone covered with sphagnum moss and wrapped with cording, satin ribbon, and tinsel. Vicki also gilded and silvered the tiny shells that decorate the tree. Scattered at its base are others that she gilded and painted with enamel paint.

"I've always had offbeat Christmas trees, and I've always used purple to decorate because it's my favorite color," Vicki explains. "Then when we moved to this house, it just didn't feel right to use reindeers and Santas, so we went tropical. It seemed more suitable and more in tune with the house."

The Deweys' tropical tastes developed after a vacation in Tahiti in 1986. "That trip changed everything," Vicki recalls. They sold their older Spanish-style home and bought this house, which she describes as "tropatech"—high-tech architecture with a tropical flavor. Designed with the humid Florida climate in mind, the concrete-block home integrates the outdoors with the interiors through window walls and sliding glass doors.

In keeping with their new style, the couple began an "under the sea" Christmas tree, on which colorful, hand-carved fish from Bali swim among other ornaments that suggest beach activities. "We stumbled onto the carved fish and purchased some of the coral and sea fans," Vicki says, "but the idea really grew when our friends found out about our tree and started giving us ornaments."

Vicki, an artist, also made some of the ornaments herself. She gilded shells, collected from strolls along the beach, with gold and silver leaf and painted designs on others in cool, ice cream colors. Sea fans, starfish, blue-green tinsel to represent seaweed, and tiny white lights complete the underwater fantasy.

The theme also carries over to the dining table, which Vicki sets with shell-patterned china and a porcelain clamshell filled with blue Christmas balls. English "crackers," candles, and foil star garland continue the purple and blue scheme.

Throughout the house, Vicki's paintings of dreamy tropical settings add color to the neutral background. The one over the buffet in the dining room is atypical in that it includes words. It bears her favorite holiday message: "Peace on Earth and under the Sea." "There are a couple of underlying themes in this piece," Vicki explains. "Stars can be found in the sea as well as in the sky, and Jesus was a fisherman of men. So it combines my love of the water with the meaning of the holiday." Like the Deweys' decorations, the painting puts a Florida spin on the celebration of the season.

Display Poinsettias with Panache

Your poinsettias will draw a second look when you present them in sacks of gold. This clever idea from Diane Hansen, owner of Harmony House Bed and Breakfast in New Bern, North Carolina, is an imaginative alternative to the red or green foil that often wraps the plastic pots in which these Christmas plants are grown. It also solves another problem that poinsettias sometimes present: The bushy top of the plant is often so much larger than its pot that it looks out of scale. Diane's plump wrappings hide the pots and balance the plants visually so that they no longer look top-heavy.

The wrappings are made from ordinary paper grocery bags. For each plant, you'll need two bags. Cut along the back center seam of each bag, down to the bottom. Cut the bottom off and open out the bag—you should have a large rectangle. Crumple the bags, then smooth them out again so that they have a crinkled texture. Spray both sides of each bag gold.

Center one opened-out bag over the other at right angles. Place the pot of flowers in a plastic-lined basket and position the basket on the center of the overlapping bags. Bring the bags up around the basket and roll the top edges over to make a collar. Tuck under the edges of the bags along the corners and bottom so that no raw edges show.

To plump the sack, stuff it with crumpled newspaper. Then tie a ribbon around the collar to hold it in place and add a bow to the front.

Above: Give extra emphasis to poinsettias by tucking the pots into plump sacks that you make from grocery bags sprayed gold.

Above: Festive swags and wreaths of chili peppers, traditional in the Southwest, garnish the entry. On the lamp, floral wire is looped through the wrought iron to secure the garland. Smaller dried materials are then hot-glued into the arrangement.

A Southwest-Style Celebration

Mike and Jodie Gallagher deck their Southwest-style halls with *chile ristra* (garlands of dried red peppers), but the *nacimiento* (manger scene) is the true centerpiece of their holiday.

"I have concentrated on the manger scene," says Jodie, "because that's what Christmas is, a celebration of Christ's birth."

The Gallaghers' home, in Houston, Texas, was built in 1929 to resemble a Basque farmhouse.

For Jodie and Mike, this house offered the ideal backdrop for their collection of Native American and Mexican art. The savory decorating style is completed by Spanish Colonial furnishings.

At Christmas, or *la Navidad* (the Nativity), Jodie adds decorations for the season with the help of floral designer Jeff Bradley. Using fresh fir, giant cones from Pacific sequoia trees, red holly and red Brazilian pepper berries, and jewel-toned

Carved Nativities, Santa Clauses, and a
Noah's Ark—all part of Jodie's collection—
go on display for Christmas. Over the mantel,
a Santa Fe angel is framed in the badge by white
oak branches, berries, and silk wired ribbon. For
the badge, chicken wire reinforces the craft foam
base that holds the floral material in place.

Above: This Native American depiction of the Nativity was sculpted by Alma Concha Loretto of the Jemes Pueblo, New Mexico. The clay Nativity and others in wood and tin represent the focus of the Gallaghers' Christmas celebration.

dried cockscomb and statice, Jeff arranges displays to complement the distinctive style of the home.

Jodie sets out folk art carvings, ethnic Santas, and carved and sculpted crèches. She is especially fond of one Nativity from New Mexico, because the Native American sculptor related the Christ child's birth to her own culture. Instead of the biblical gifts of gold, frankincense, and myrrh, the clay figures bring chili peppers, corn, and bread.

With the floral designs in place, Mike and Jodie welcome home their three children and invite other family members to join them for a working Thanksgiving weekend. Organized into three crews—lights, ornaments, and *luminarias*—they decorate the Christmas tree and line the front walk with the traditional Mexican Christmas lanterns.

La Navidad at the Gallaghers' blends their family traditions with the Southwest's ethnic flavors to create a piquant Christmas style.

Above: This soft-sculpture Christmas tree and favorite old toys add a touch of Southwest whimsy. Jodie's mother made the needlepoint tree ornaments.

Opposite: In the dining room, late 19th century Moroccan shutters are a backdrop for the centerpiece, a handmade fir garland jeweled with berries, larkspur, cockscomb, and nuts.

Above: Copper-colored chargers and copper place cards and napkin rings are easy to make and bring a warm, festive glow to your table setting.

Terrific Tablescapes to Create

Even the simplest menu can become a grand occasion if the setting is spectacular. A tablescape sets the mood for festivity—and it's a beautifully eloquent way for you to make guests feel welcome and special. We've created four tablescapes to inspire you. One is easy, inexpensive, and very merry. The other three, based on the themes of marbleizing, music, and copper, let you put your craft skills to work.

THE WARMTH OF COPPER

Set a gleaming table with copper-toned chargers and copper candlesticks, place card holders, and napkin rings. To make the chargers, apply red spray paint to plain wooden plates. Allow the paint to dry and then lightly mist the plates with gold spray paint. Copper tooling foil for the place card holders is easy to work with and can be found at art supply shops. Most of the supplies for the candlesticks and napkin rings come from the hardware store. (Instructions are on pages 63-64.)

A PERFECTLY MARBLEOUS SETTING

Using paint to simulate marble is an art that has enjoyed periodic revivals since at least the second century B.C. Today you'll see the look of stone on everything from baseboards to bedsheets. We've used a simplified version of the art to create an elegant setting for a holiday dinner, with marbleized place mats, napkin rings, and candle shades. Roses made of gold lamé and nestled on braids of ivy add luscious sparkle to the table. (See page 62 for instructions on how to marbleize and how to make the projects.)

58

The simple technique of marbleizing gives elegant results. Make your own place mats and napkin rings, with candle shades to match. Use glass votives as vases for diminutive bouquets for each guest, and combine gold lamé roses with fresh ivy to decorate the center of the table.

Start with one motif—a French horn ornament—and build on it to make a thoroughly theme-oriented tablescape. Sheet music serves as place mats.

MAKING MERRY MUSIC

French horn ornaments were the starting point for this tablescape. The ornaments themselves serve as napkin rings and inspired the motif on the painted napkins. To carry the musical theme further, we used inexpensive sheet music for place mats and hunting-horn ornaments for place card holders. For the centerpiece, we borrowed a real French horn, but you could also assemble decorative brass horns of different sizes. Combine them with a few fresh flowers and greenery for a show-stopping focal point.

Decorating the napkins is easy—just use fabric-painting pens, ivory or white polyester-cotton blend napkins, and the pattern on page 145. Wash and dry the napkins first, to remove the sizing. Transfer the pattern to one corner of the napkin. Outline the entire motif with gold and then paint the bow red and one horn gold. After the paint dries, heat-set the design according to the instructions on the paint pens.

Left: Use paint pens to turn inexpensive polyester-cotton blend napkins into custom-made table linens.

Gather all of your candlesticks and wrap them with curling ribbon to give a festive look to the table. Wrap the napkin rings and the stems of your crystal too.

CURLING RIBBONS AND CANDLES

Inexpensive curling ribbon—yards of it—transforms a table into a delightfully high-spirited setting for a holiday dinner. The key is to wrap everything you can with the ribbon—the candlesticks, the napkin rings, the stems of water and wine glasses—to create a froth of festive curls.

Cut ribbon into pieces about 2 yards long or less, depending on the size of what you're wrapping. Double a piece of ribbon and wrap it around the napkin ring or along the length of the glass stem or candlestick, ending with a knot and leaving 6-inch tails. Cut another piece of curling ribbon about 1½ yards long and loop it around your hand as if making a bow. Pinch the looped ribbon in the middle and tie it to the ribbon-wrapped object. Then, to make the froth of curls, clip the loops, hold them firmly at the center, and curl the ribbon ends with scissors or a knife.

(To remove the ribbon wrappings, just use a sharp utility knife to cut them away. Pile all the curled ribbon in a bowl with glass balls for another happy decoration, or add the ringlets to the branches of your tree.)

MARBLEIZED PLACE MATS, NAPKIN RINGS, AND CANDLE SHADES

To make the place mats, use ordinary awning canvas or artist's canvas. (If you use artist's canvas, you'll need to seal it with gesso before painting it.) Cut the canvas into rectangles 14 inches by 16½ inches and press under a 1-inch seam all around. Miter the corners and glue the seams to the back of the place mat. When the glue is dry, apply the base coat and marbleize according to the instructions below.

The napkin rings are simply 2¼-inch-diameter wooden curtain rings with the screw eyes removed. The metal candle shades can be purchased with a matte black finish, so all you have to do is apply the green and white paints and veining.

HOW TO MARBLEIZE

You'll need acrylic paints in white, black, and 2 shades of green. You'll also need FolkArt Thickener, FolkArt Extender, a sponge, feathers, and gold-leaf paint.

Paint the project with a base coat of black and let it dry. Using a disposable pie plate as a palette, carefully pour a thin line of light green paint in a circle in the plate. Pour twice as much dark green and ¼ as much white on top of and around the light green. Then squeeze 1½ circles of thickener and 1 of extender on top of the paints. Tilt the palette to mingle the colors.

Use a natural sponge, or tear small chunks from 1 side and all edges of a synthetic one to make the surface irregular. Lightly place the torn side of the sponge on the paints so that it picks up a thin coat of all 3 colors; then press it on the base-coated project. (It's a good idea to test the paint mixture on a piece of paper first.) Use a pecking motion and be careful not to clump the paint thickly.

Let the paint dry thoroughly. To apply the veining, squeeze 1 part white, 1 part thickener, and 2 parts extender in a clean pie plate. Tilt to mingle the ingredients. Drag a feather through the mixture, then pull it across the surface of the project with an irregular motion to create thick and thin

lines of white. It may take some practice to make the veins look naturalistic. Slant all lines in the same direction, but not precisely parallel to each other, and vary both the thickness and the length. When the veining dries, use gold-leaf paint and a feather to apply accents. After the project is completely dry, spray it with a protective acrylic sealer.

GOLD LAME ROSES

To make the fabric roses, cut 1 yard of 45-inch-wide tissue lamé into strips according to the diagram below. Each strip will make 1 rose. Fold 1 strip in half lengthwise. On the narrow end of the strip, fold the top corner down to meet the raw edge at a 90-degree angle.

Bend 1 end of an 18-inch-long piece of #24 (medium-weight) florist's wire to form a hook. Using the wire like a needle, thread the opposite end back and forth through the length of the fabric ½ inch from the raw edges, beginning at the narrow end and making "stitches" about ½ inch long. Push the fabric onto the wire to make soft gathers. Secure them on the wire by bending it in a U shape several inches from the end.

To shape the rose, grasp the wire at the beginning with needle-nose pliers and wrap the fabric strip tightly around the tip in a circular pattern, forming the center of the rose with the narrow end of the fabric strip and the petals with the wide end. Twist the ends of the wire to form a stem.

To make a calyx, cut a 4-inch square of green tissue lamé. Push the stem through the center of the square, gather the fabric around the base of the rose, and secure it by wrapping it with the stem wire.

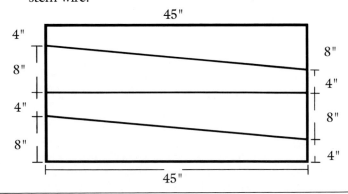

Above: Copper tubing and brass fittings from the plumbing department of a hardware store combine with brass bases from a lamp shop to create these distinctive candlesticks.

COPPER CANDLESTICKS

Materials (for set of 3):
pipe cutter or hack saw
14" (¾") copper tubing
2 feet (⅜") threaded pipe
steel wool
6 (⅜") nuts
6 (¾"-diameter) washers with ⅜"
   center hole
3 (¾"-to-½") copper reducing
   couplings
3 (1") brass check rings or vase rings
3 (½") copper sweat unions with
   brass nuts
3 (¾") copper female sweat adapters
3 (2½"-square) brass lamp bases
pliers
epoxy glue or cold weld
3 (1") brass male threaded rings (from
   hose repair kit)

With pipe cutter or hack saw, from copper tubing, cut a 6⅞" length for 12" candlestick, a 3⅞" length for 9" candlestick, and a 2½" length for

7½" candlestick. (Be sure cuts are straight; otherwise candlesticks will be lopsided.)

From threaded pipe, cut a 10½" length for 12" candlestick, a 7½" length for 9" candlestick, and a 6" length for 7½" candlestick. With steel wool, lightly rub off any burrs from cut ends.

Following diagram below, assemble hardware, copper tubing, and lamp parts on threaded pipe. Align parts; tighten top and bottom nuts with pliers. Using epoxy glue or cold weld, secure brass ring from hose repair kit to top of reducing coupling.

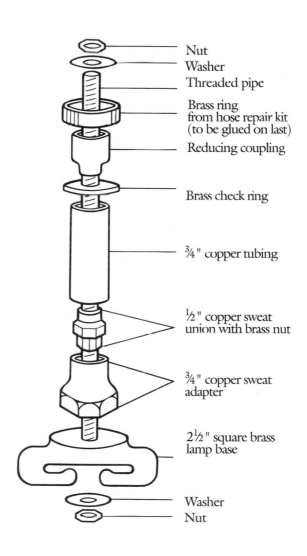

Nut
Washer
Threaded pipe
Brass ring
from hose repair kit
(to be glued on last)
Reducing coupling

Brass check ring

¾" copper tubing

½" copper sweat
union with brass nut

¾" copper sweat
adapter

2½" square brass
lamp base

Washer
Nut

COPPER PLACE CARD HOLDERS

For each place card holder, you will need a 6-inch by 4¾-inch piece of cardboard, 40-gauge copper tooling foil, assorted acrylic jewels, a pencil, a Phillips screwdriver or dry ballpoint pen, and a hot-glue gun and glue sticks.

Cut a 7-inch by 5¾-inch piece of copper foil. Fold the cardboard in half widthwise; then unfold it and center it on the foil. Fold the edges of the foil over the cardboard and miter the corners.

To make the stars, transfer some of the patterns for stars on the copper picture frames on page 140 to the foil and cut out. Working on a soft surface, such as a towel or dishcloth, stipple the stars using the tip of the screwdriver or the ball-point pen.

Arrange the stars at the corners of the place card holder, being careful to leave enough room to center the card between the points of the stars. Use the hot-glue gun to glue the stars in place; then glue an acrylic jewel to the center of each star.

COPPER NAPKIN RINGS

To make the star napkin rings, you will need 18- and 24-gauge copper wire, scraps of 40-gauge copper tooling foil, assorted acrylic jewels, and a hot-glue gun and glue sticks.

Begin by cutting 3 (16-inch) pieces of 18-gauge wire. Holding the 3 wires together as 1, start at 1 end and wrap the bundle with a length of 24-gauge wire, allowing about ¼ inch between wraps (see photograph).

Form a 2-inch-diameter circle at 1 end of the wrapped wire and secure it by wrapping it with 24-gauge wire. Bend the remaining wire to make a spiral as shown in the photograph.

Use the patterns on page 140 to cut a large star from copper tooling foil. Texture it as for the place card stars and make a small hole in 1 point. Thread a 4-inch piece of 24-gauge wire through the hole to form a loop; then secure the loop to the end of the napkin ring. Use the hot-glue gun to glue an acrylic jewel to the center of the star.

A Tree That Glows

Treasured ornaments, from seashell angels to paper Santas, are illuminated in the glow of this warm and starry Christmas tree.

Julianne McClure, interior designer, decorated the tree for her parents, Warren and Pat Chilton of Marietta, Georgia. Four elements, combined with her family's collected ornaments, create this radiant design—strings of miniature red lights, a custom-made ribbon topper, gold foil star garland, and red-glittered *ting ting* (a 24-inch-long dried ornamental grass that looks like a wispy stick).

Julianne began by wrapping the tree branches in strings of miniature red lights. She then hung the ornaments, distributing the shapes and colors evenly over the tree.

For the centerpiece of the ribbon topper, Julianne chose a papier-mâché angel; however, any showy Christmas figure could be used. From wide wire-edged lamé ribbon she made two bows— one gold and one red—that were large enough to frame the angel. Nesting the red bow into the gold with florist's wire, she then set the angel into the red bow. She wired this to the tree and trailed several red ribbons down from the topper.

The foil star garland laces in and out of the tree branches. Julianne gently uncoiled the purchased garland, retaining the loose corkscrew curls. Then she cut the garland every three or four loops to make shorter lengths. Working in a vertical pattern, she attached the garland to the tree by crimping one end to a branch, weaving in and out of the branches and crimping the other end to another branch.

To finish, Julianne poked long, slender *ting ting* into the tree from top to bottom. Even in daylight, this delicate treatment creates a warm, glowing halo around the entire tree.

Above right: Woven with shining star garland and tiny red lights, this Christmas tree shows off a family's treasured collection of ornaments.

Right: Glittered ting ting, *a dried ornamental grass, creates the illusion of a glowing halo around this noble fir.*

Above: Big bows of wired ribbon mark the ends and center of the mantel, and short lengths of wired ribbon are twisted around the garland so that they seem to wrap it. The artificial greenery makes a flexible, sturdy foundation for strings of twinkling white lights, clusters of glass balls, and wired star garland.

66

Above: Red velvet ribbon with gold wired edges creates a lively, swirling line through this mantel decoration. Fresh garland and magnolia leaves form the base for the arrangement; fresh and artificial fruits, pinecones, and gilded lotus pods are simply balanced on the mantel or tucked into the garland.

Beribboned Mantels

Wrap your mantel with ribbons—wired ribbons, that is. Now available in a wide variety of fabrics, this ribbon can be furled, curled, twisted, and pinched to give dimension and excitement to arrangements. It's expensive—but you might think of it as a Christmas investment, something you'll use over and over, year after year.

Red velvet ribbon with a gold wired edge gives the mantel above a rich, baroque look. Streamers from the bow at the center sweep back to the garland on either side, where the pineapples help hold them in place. Additional lengths of ribbon tie gilded wheat to the topiaries and swirl around their tops. For a mantel treatment like this one, designer Michele Bray Klutts advises using a length of ribbon that is three times the length of the mantel. That way, you can swag or loop the

ribbon from one end to the other, tucking it back into the greenery at intervals and leaving enough fullness to shape it into soft curves. To achieve the windswept effect around the topiaries, Michele and homeowner Joanne Pinkett molded the ribbon around their hands.

The mantel opposite shows another way to use wired ribbon effectively. Big bows mark the ends and center of the swag. Instead of simply wrapping the entire garland with more ribbon, designer Bill Whisenant achieved a much livelier result by using shorter lengths of ribbon and pinching and twisting them so that they appear to spiral around the greenery without actually doing so. Wired foil star garland in a variety of colors adds a sparkling, gestural line that enhances the festive effect.

Crochet a Garland Of Stars

These garlands of crocheted stars are so quick and easy to work up that you'll want to make them for trimming your mantel and stairs as well as the tree. The gold garland below is crocheted with a size 10 cotton thread that has metallic accents woven in. The samples at bottom show the variety of pleasing effects you can get using heavier (size 3) pearl cotton and metallic embroidery thread. The two threads are held together as one and crocheted with a size 6 steel crochet hook.

Above: If you work the pattern using size 3 pearl cotton, you will need 4½ yards of thread per 2-inch star.

Top: These 6-foot-long garlands are crocheted with size 10 crochet cotton.

Materials:
size 10 crochet cotton with gold metallic accents: 2 (100-yard) balls gold
size 3 steel crochet hook (or size to obtain gauge)
tapestry needle
spray starch (optional)

Note: Each star requires approximately 3¼ yards of thread. The models contain 36 stars each and are each approximately 6 feet long.

Gauge: Star = 2".

First star: Leave a 4" tail of thread at beg and work first rnd of sts over it. **Rnd 1:** Ch 5, join with a sl st to form a ring. **Rnd 2:** Ch 2, * ch 7, dc in ring, rep from * 3 times more, sl st in top of beg ch-2. **Rnd 3:** * (Sc in lp, ch 1) 3 times, (dc in lp, ch 1) twice, (sc in lp, ch 1) twice, sc in same lp, rep from * around, end with sl st in first sc. Fasten off.

Second star: Rep rnds 1 and 2 of first star. **Rnd 3 (joining rnd):** * (Sc in lp, ch 1) 3 times, dc in lp, with wrong sides facing, hold first star behind 2nd star, insert hook in ch-1 sp between 2 dc, yo and pull up a lp, yo and pull through both lps, dc in same lp on 2nd star, (ch 1, sc in lp) 3 times, end with sl st in first sc. Fasten off.

Rep to make and join stars for desired length of garland.

Finishing: Use tapestry needle to weave in all yarn ends. Place garland between 2 terry cloth towels and lightly press with a steam iron. (Do not place iron directly on garland.) Apply spray starch to both sides of garland, if desired.

Crochet Abbreviations:
beg–begin(ning)
ch–chain
dc–double crochet
lp(s)–loop(s)
rep–repeat
rnd(s)–round(s)
sc–single crochet
sl st–slip stitch
sp–space
st(s)–stitch(es)
yo–yarn over

Christmas Bazaar

Emboss Copper for Starry Frames

You'll want to make these copper frames as gifts for everyone on your list. Tooling the copper is easy, and the random star pattern gives the frame a festive look that suits the season but isn't limited to it. Put glass in the opening to display a picture or insert a mirror for a handsome accessory with a Southwest flavor.

Materials:
For each frame:
patterns on page 140
tracing paper
graphite paper
band saw or jigsaw
wood glue
wood clamp
sandpaper
gold semigloss enamel
paintbrush
20" square of corrugated cardboard
masking tape
dry ballpoint pen or dull pencil for
    embossing
sharp utility knife
tack hammer
packing tape

For large frame:
8½" x 10½" piece of ½" plywood
12" x 14" (36-gauge) copper
    tooling foil
4 (7") pieces (¼" x ¾") screen molding
    for back supports
10 brass escutcheon tacks
18 brass upholstery nails
10 (¾") flathead tacks
1 sawtooth picture hanger
1 (5" x 7") piece of glass
1 (5" x 7") piece of corrugated
    cardboard

For small frame:
6½" x 8⅝" piece of ½" plywood
10" x 12" (36-gauge) copper
    tooling foil
2 (7") pieces and 2 (3") pieces (¼" x ¾")
    screen molding for back supports
10 brass escutcheon tacks
12 brass upholstery nails
10 (¾") flathead tacks
1 sawtooth picture hanger
1 (3" x 5") piece of glass
1 (3" x 5") piece of corrugated
    cardboard

Transfer pattern to tracing paper. Use graphite paper to transfer outline for center opening to plywood. With band saw or jigsaw, cut through

frame to outline of center opening. Follow outline with saw and exit along same cut as entered. Remove center. Put a small amount of wood glue into cut in frame. Clamp frame and let glue dry. Sand all surfaces. With gold enamel, paint inside edges of center opening.

Lay copper foil on 20"-square of corrugated cardboard and secure edges with masking tape. Center traced pattern on copper; secure with tape. Using pen or pencil, trace over stars and dots, pressing down firmly to emboss copper. Mark outside and inside corners of pattern on foil and mark arch for large frame. Remove pattern and tape. Turn foil over.

Position wooden frame on foil, matching outside and inside corner marks. Fold outside edges of foil around frame to back, mitering corners. Using brass escutcheon tacks, secure edges of copper foil to back of frame.

Working from front of frame, insert utility knife at 1 inside corner mark of center opening. Trim copper out of center opening by pressing knife against frame edge as you cut. To secure copper on front, tack copper to wood around edge of opening with brass upholstery nails.

To hold picture in place, mark placement lines for back supports on back of frame by drawing a line 1¾" from each outside edge of frame. Align inside edge of each back support with placement line and nail in place with flathead tacks.

Attach picture hanger to top support. Insert glass and photograph (or, if you prefer, a mirror) and cardboard backing. Secure backing to supports with packing tape.

71

A Coppery Christmas

Copper has a ruddy glow that's rich, warm, and inviting. It looks good with gold or brass, and when it weathers, it develops the verdigris finish that's popular now. Verdigris inspired the sponge-painted tree at left. The combination of brass and copper and the technique for making vine wreaths suggested the brass-and-copper wreath at right. Start with a circle of wire, and weave the wire in and out around it, just as you would honeysuckle vine. Hang this sparkly wreath on the tree, or make a set to use as Christmassy napkin rings. The embossed ornament is easy to make, using copper tooling foil. Its gleaming surface will catch the light and make your Christmas tree shine.

SPONGED COPPER TREE

Materials:
pattern on page 141
3 (9¼" x 10½") sheets of medium-weight
  craft copper
hole punches: round, star-shaped
sponge
acrylic paints: green, light green
aluminum pie plate
cold weld

Transfer pattern to copper and cut out to make 3 trees. Using hole punches, make round and star-shaped holes in branches and body of trees.

Pull out bits of sponge from surface and edges so that surface of sponge is irregular. Squeeze a small amount of green paint into plate. Dip sponge into paint and sponge lightly in a random manner over 1 side of each tree. Let dry. Repeat with light green paint. Let dry. Repeat on remaining sides of trees.

Referring to photograph, fold each tree along center line to form an angle. Following manufacturer's instructions, use cold weld to attach the 3 trees along the fold.

BRASS-AND-COPPER WIRE WREATH

Materials (for 1 wreath):
3 yards of 18-gauge copper wire
2 yards of 18-gauge brass wire
9 (4-mm) gold pearl beads
9 (4-mm) silver pearl beads
½ yard (¼"-wide) green satin ribbon

With copper wire, form a 2"-diameter circle, interlacing end to secure. Weave wire around circle 2 times (as you would a grapevine wreath) to establish shape. Referring to photograph, continue wrapping wire around wreath, making loops perpendicular to initial shape. Loops will not be uniform but should be spaced to give an overall effect of fullness.

With brass wire, bend 1 end and hook into copper loops at any point on wreath. Wrap wire around wreath in loops as with copper. As you make loops, slide a silver or gold bead onto brass wire every 2 or 3 loops so that the next loop holds it in place. Alternate silver and gold beads. Hide end of wire in loops.

Cut ribbon in half. Slip 1 piece through loops at top of wreath and tie in a bow. For hanger, slip remaining piece through loop behind bow and knot ends.

ROUND EMBOSSED ORNAMENT

Materials (for 1 ornament):
pattern on page 141
3"-diameter cardboard circle
4"-diameter circle of 40-gauge copper tooling foil
tracing paper
dry ballpoint pen or dull pencil
5" (¼"-wide) green satin ribbon
hot-glue gun and glue stick
2"-diameter circle of 40-gauge copper tooling foil

Center cardboard circle on copper circle. Clip curves to edge of cardboard and fold excess copper to back of cardboard.

Transfer pattern to tracing paper and center on right side of ornament. Using pen or pencil, trace over all details, pressing down firmly to emboss copper.

To make hanger, fold ribbon in half. Glue ends of ribbon to back of ornament. Center and glue remaining foil circle to back of ornament.

We've Put a Bunny On the Moon!

This whimsical ornament recalls childhood dreams of swinging on a star and carrying moonbeams home in a jar. The big-footed bunny bouncing on a velour crescent moon adds a touch of fun to Christmas tree branches or your child's special present.

Materials:
patterns on page 148
2 (6") squares of white velour
water-soluble fabric marker
stuffing
2 black seed beads
pink embroidery floss
light pink fabric paint
small paintbrush
1 (¼"-diameter) white pom-pom
2 (6") squares of blue velour
threads to match fabrics
tiny silver sequin stars
white or pearl seed beads
⅝" silver sequin star
10" (⅛"-wide) white satin
  ribbon

Note: Velour nap should run in downward direction.

Transfer bunny to wrong side of 1 square of white velour. Cut back slit as indicated on pattern. With right sides facing and raw edges aligned, stitch 2 velour squares together along traced stitching line. Trim seam allowance ¹⁄₁₆" from seam. Turn through slit. Mark facial features and toes. Lightly stuff bunny. (It may be helpful to use a knitting needle.) Do not stuff ears.

Using an 18" length of white thread, slipstitch slit closed from bottom to top. Do not cut thread. To shape neck, reinsert needle into bunny at top of slit and bring out on right side of neck. Reinsert needle close to point of exit, draw through neck, and bring out on left side. Reinsert again and bring out on right side, drawing thread tight to define neck. Take a small stitch to secure thread but do not cut. Bring needle and thread around front of neck and insert needle into left side of neck. Draw through to right side and pull tight, creating a chin. Do not cut thread.

Continue with same thread to attach eyes and shape face as follows. Facing front of bunny, insert needle into left side of neck and bring out at right eye mark. Thread a bead onto needle, reinsert needle at same eye mark, and bring out at left side of neck. Keeping thread taut, bring thread around front under chin to right side of neck. Insert needle and bring out at left eye mark. Thread a bead onto needle, reinsert needle at same eye mark, and bring out at right side of neck, pulling thread tight. Secure and cut thread.

Using 3 strands of pink floss, make several small straightstitches for nose.

Using fabric paint, paint inner ears.

To make toes, refer to pattern and pull needle up through bottom of foot. Bring out at point A, keeping thread taut. Loop thread around outside edge of foot and bring needle up through point A again, pulling thread tight. Loop around edge of foot, insert needle at A and out at B. Continue this process for remaining toes, securing thread after last toe. Repeat for other foot. Stitch pom-pom to back of bunny for tail.

Transfer moon to wrong side of 1 square of blue velour. With right sides facing and raw edges aligned, stitch squares of blue velour together along stitching line, leaving open where indicated on pattern. Trim seam allowance ⅛" from seam. Turn and stuff. Slipstitch opening closed.

Referring to photograph, stitch stars and beads on front and back of moon as desired, bringing needle through each star and bead and then pushing needle back through star. Sew ⅝" star between bunny's paws.

Referring to photograph, position bunny on moon, being sure nap on moon runs downward. Tack feet and head to moon.

For hanger, fold ribbon in half, tack fold to top of ornament, and knot ends.

Clever Ideas for Recycling Christmas Cards

Even with rising postage costs, sending Christmas cards is still one of the most popular holiday traditions in America. If you're like most people, after the holidays you probably find yourself wondering what you should do with the cards you've received. They're too pretty to throw away, but who has room to store all of them? Here are several quick and easy ideas for putting old cards to new use.

One of the easiest ways to recycle old cards is to cut the fronts off and use them next year as postcards and gift tags. If a card has a decorative border, you can cut out the center for a gift tag and use the border as a handsome mat for a holiday photograph. Use a craft knife to cut out the center of the card so that the border will remain intact. You may need to trim the edges slightly so that the card will fit a standard-size picture frame.

If you have an assortment of cards, use them to decorate a cigar box for a container that's a gift in itself. This is an easy holiday project for children.

Cut shapes from cards, glue them on the sides and top of the box with Mod Podge glue, and then varnish the entire box to protect the surface and add some shine. Top it with a big bow and fill it with homemade cookies for a perfect gift for the teacher.

For a gift that looks like something from a museum catalog, decorate a purchased, lidded wooden box with a card depicting a reproduction of a painting (see page 25). Paint the box the desired color—we used gold enamel. After the paint dries, glue the card front to the lid. Apply 2 coats of super spar varnish for a glossy, durable finish.

Christmas cards are also the starting point for a trio of clever projects: a tiny box, a jigsaw puzzle, and holiday jewelry. Use a large card to make the box for tiny treasures. Enlarge the pattern below, transfer it to the back of a card front, and cut it out. Fold and tape the box together where indicated; then add ribbon and a bow.

For puzzle-loving friends, fill the box with a jigsaw puzzle greeting. Trim the card front, write your message on the back, and then have the card laminated at an office supply or copy store. Draw puzzle pieces on the back and cut them out with scissors or a craft knife.

For a stylish seasonal pin, begin with a basic shape cut from a card. Varnish the shape, and then add scraps of paper, beads, sequins, pearls, ribbons, rhinestones, and whatever else you might have on hand. Glue a bar pin to the back, near the top of the pin.

Used wrapping paper can also be recycled. Apply it to ordinary clay flowerpots to create wonderful containers for gifts. Tear the paper into 1- to 1½-inch pieces. With a stiff paintbrush, apply Gloss-Lustre Mod Podge glue to a small area on the pot. Position pieces of wrapping paper at varying angles on the glue and brush more glue over them. Be sure to apply the glue generously and to overlap the paper pieces. Work from the bottom of the pot to the top and over the rim to about 1 inch inside. Apply a final coat of glue to create a hard, shiny finish. Larger pots are perfect for poinsettias or Christmas cactus. Smaller pots offer a clever way to present a variety of gifts. Stuff the pot with colorful tissue paper and nestle a surprise inside.

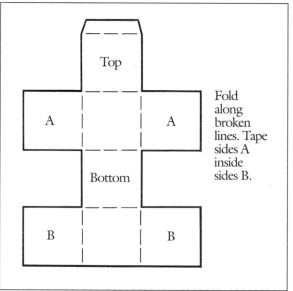

Craft Wise Men From Wood

Painted in royal colors, these three stately kings stand with outstretched arms. Place a votive candle or small gift on each tray for a majestic mantel or table display.

Materials (for 3 kings):
patterns on pages 142-45
graphite paper
12" x 76" piece of ¾" pine shelving
band saw
router with 45° mitering bit
**   or table saw**
3 (4" x 6") pieces of ½" pine (for trays)
sandpaper
satin varnish
acrylic paints: black, yellow, turquoise,
**   white, pink, purple, light flesh, dark**
**   flesh, dark red, red, cream, brown**
paintbrushes
wood glue
1¼" (#18) wire brads
wood filler

Using graphite paper, transfer patterns to pine shelving and cut out with band saw. For each king, cut 1 (6") square for bottom base piece and 1 piece (4¼" x 4½") for top base piece.

Using router with 45° mitering bit or table saw, cut a beveled edge along top 3 sides of all bases and trays.

Sand all pieces, including edges. Using graphite paper, transfer all details onto wooden figures. Apply 1 coat of satin varnish to all pieces and let dry. Lightly sand. Paint all bottom base pieces black. Paint top base piece as shown in photograph. Referring to photograph and patterns, paint figures and arms.

To attach arms, referring to photograph, center top of 1 arm ¼" above shoulder on each side of 1 king, positioning hands at right angle to body. Glue arms to body. Secure with wire brads.

Countersink brad heads, fill in with wood filler, sand, and touch up paint. Repeat for remaining kings.

Using brads, attach tray to hands of figures with unbeveled edge of tray toward body. Countersink

brad heads, fill in with wood filler, and sand. Referring to photograph, paint trays.

For each king, center body piece on unbeveled edge of bottom base piece, aligning back of body with edge of base, and glue in place. Referring to photograph, position top base piece in front of body piece with unbeveled edge abutting body. Glue; secure bases from underneath, using brads. Apply 1-2 coats of varnish to figures, allowing to dry between coats.

Sculpt a Family
Of Carolers

This little family of carolers and their snowman are made from a sculpturing compound that stays soft until you bake it in the oven. It's so easy to work with that children can help.

Half of a 2-pound box of flesh-colored Super Sculpey is more than enough to make the figures shown in the photograph. Making them is simply a matter of shaping the compound into balls and snake-like rolls and pressing the pieces together. Use a toothpick to score lines for clothing details and to make each caroler's mouth.

To make the carolers' bodies, form a ½-inch-diameter roll. Cut a 2½- to 3-inch length for each tall caroler and a 1½- to 2-inch length for each short one. Shape the body so that 1 end is narrower than the other. For each head, roll a ½- to ¾-inch-diameter ball and secure it to the narrow end of the body with a piece of toothpick.

For the arms, form a thin roll of compound and cut pieces 1 to 2 inches long. Press them in place on the sides of the body, bending them at the elbow to hold a hymnbook or drum.

To make the drum, roll the compound into a ball and flatten opposite ends. Secure it to the body with a piece of toothpick pushed into the body below the hands. For the drumsticks, push a piece of toothpick into each hand.

To make the hymnbook, form a thin, flat square of compound, bend it slightly in the center, and position it on the hands.

To make the hair, you can either shape a small amount of compound into a flat circle, press it on the head, and comb it with a toothpick to create texture; or press the compound through a garlic press and position the strands on the head.

For the snowman, roll 3 balls in graduated sizes and secure them to each other with pieces of toothpick. Shape the crown of the hat from a small ball of compound; shape the brim from a flat circle. Secure the brim and crown to the head with a piece of toothpick. Form a thin roll of compound and flatten it to make the scarf; use pieces of toothpick for the arms and nose.

Following the manufacturer's instructions, bake the figures in the oven. After they cool, paint them as desired with acrylic paints. Draw the eyes and the snowman's mouth with markers and apply blush to the carolers' cheeks, using a cotton swab.

Appliqué a "Sleepy Reindeer" Stocking

This easy appliqué stocking features Santa's chief helper, tucked in bed and fast asleep after a long night's work. Polyester suede, velveteen, and wool give the reindeer and his blanket touchable texture. When you cut out the piece for the blanket, use the selvage edge for the blanket top to create the effect of fringe.

Materials:
patterns on pages 146-47
⅓ yard (45"-wide) double-sided pre-quilted muslin
⅓ yard of paper-backed fusible web
scraps of polyester suede: tan, medium brown, dark brown
scraps of velveteen: red, black
1 (10½" x 7") piece of red wool plaid
1 (3½" x 17") strip of sherpa
dimensional fabric paint: glossy black
craft glue

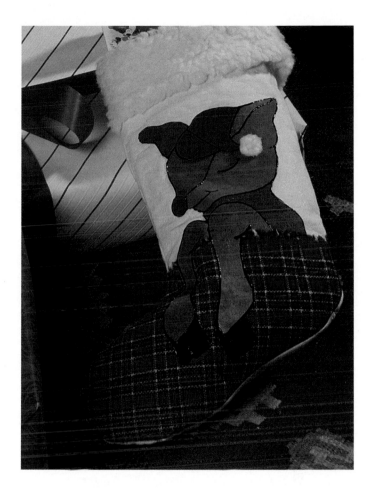

Note: Add ½" seam allowance to stocking and blanket patterns. Suede nap should run in downward direction.

Transfer stocking pattern to muslin and cut 2.

Following manufacturer's instructions, fuse web to wrong side of suede and velveteen scraps and wool plaid. Transfer appliqué patterns to paper side of web and cut out as follows: face from tan suede; head and legs from medium brown; chest and right ear from dark brown; hat and nose from red velveteen; hooves from black velveteen; pom-pom for hat from sherpa. For blanket, use stocking pattern (up to blanket placement line) to make pattern, adding ½" seam allowance to outside edge; cut 1 from wool plaid.

Referring to patterns and photograph for placement and following manufacturer's instructions, fuse appliqué pieces to right side of 1 stocking piece in this order: blanket, chest, legs (tucking tops under fringe), hooves, face, head, nose, right ear, hat. Referring to photograph, outline all pattern pieces and draw eye and mouth with dimensional fabric paint. Let dry. Glue pom-pom to tip of hat.

To assemble stocking, with right sides facing and raw edges aligned, sew stocking front to back, leaving top open. Clip curves but do not turn. To make hanger loop, from muslin, cut a 1½" x 6½" strip. Fold under ¼" on each long edge and press; fold in half lengthwise, with wrong sides facing, and topstitch along long open edge. Press.

For cuff, from sherpa, cut a 3½" x 14" strip. With right sides facing, fold strip in half widthwise and stitch ends.

To join loop and cuff to stocking, with raw edges aligned, fold loop in half and pin to wrong side of stocking back near seam. With right side of cuff facing wrong side of stocking and raw edges aligned, pin cuff to top of stocking. Stitch around top of stocking. Turn stocking to right side; turn down cuff.

Knit a Pair Of Feline Pals

A woolly combination of knits and "purrls," these knitted kittens are full of "purrsonality." Knit them to use as decorating accents or to give as the "purrfect" gift that a child will love to cuddle.

Materials (for 2 dolls):
diagram, charts, and color key on page 84
worsted-weight wool: 2 oz. of red, 2 oz.
    of gray, ½ oz. each of white and green
    (for boy); 2 oz. of red, 3 oz. of gray,
    ½ oz. each of white and green
    (for girl)
4 (size 7) double-pointed needles
    (or size to obtain gauge)
stitch markers
stitch holder
stuffing
tapestry needle
felt scraps: gold, black, pink
thread to match fabrics
embroidery floss: white, black
black carpet thread
size G crochet hook

Finished Size: Approximately 14" tall.
  Gauge: 9 sts and 14 rows = 2" in St st.
  Note: Work in St st throughout. To change colors, wrap old yarn over new so that no holes occur.
  Boy Kitty Legs: With gray, cast on 10 sts. Slip a marker on needle after last st to indicate end of rnd. Arrange on dpn, connect and work in the rnd. K around. * K 1, inc 1, rep from * around (20 sts). Work even until piece measures 2" from beg. Change to red and work even until piece measures 5" from beg. Place sts on stitch holder. Make another leg as before; leave sts on needles. To join legs and beg body: Place marker on needle to indicate beg of rnd. K 10 sts, k 20 sts of first leg from holder, k 10 rem sts. Rearrange sts on needles. Work even on these 40 sts for 2 more rnds.

To leave space for tail: K 28. With scrap yarn of contrasting color, k 4. Place these 4 sts back on left-hand needle and k 12 with red. Work even until piece measures 2½" from beg of body. Change to green and k 3 rnds for waistband. To divide for armholes: Change to red, cast on 1 st

for seam allowance, k 20, cast on 1 st. Place rem 20 sts on stitch holder. Work back and forth on 22 sts in St st for 2¼". Bind off loosely. Rep for other side.

Arms (make 2): With white, cast on 20 sts. Slip a marker on needle to indicate end of rnd.

Arrange on dpn, connect and work in the rnd. Work even for 2¼". Follow chart for sleeve design for 4 rnds. Change to gray. Work even until piece measures 4" from beg. K 2 tog around. Thread yarn through rem 10 sts, pull tightly and secure.

Head: With gray, cast on 40 sts. Slip a marker on needle to indicate end of rnd. Arrange on dpn, connect and work in the rnd. Work even until piece measures 3½" from beg. To divide for ears: K 8, place next 24 sts on stitch holder, k 8. K 1 rnd on these 16 sts. K 6, ssk, k 2 tog, k 6. K 1 rnd even. K 5, ssk, k 2 tog, k 5. K 4, ssk, k 2 tog, k 4. K 2 tog, k 1, ssk, k 2 tog, k 1, ssk. Thread yarn through rem 6 sts, pull tightly and secure. Leaving 4 sts at center front and center back of head on holder, put rem 16 sts back on needles and complete other ear as before. When second ear is completed, graft the center 8 sts tog for top of head.

Girl Kitty: Work as for boy kitty, but use gray only to make legs and lower body. Work up to, but not including, green waistband and place sts on stitch holder.

Skirt: With red, cast on 56 sts. Slip a marker on needle to indicate end of rnd. Arrange on dpn, connect and work in the rnd. Work k 1, p 1 ribbing for 2 rnds. Follow chart for skirt design for 9 rnds. With red, k even until piece measures 4" from beg. (K 5, k 2 tog) around. (K 4, k 2 tog) around. To join skirt to body: Slip body piece inside skirt piece. * Place 1 body st from holder onto needle in front of next skirt st. With green, k 2 tog (the red skirt st and the gray body st), rep from * around. Work 2 more rnds even in green. Change to red, divide for armholes and complete body as for boy kitty.

Arms (make 2): Work as for boy kitty except work white for 1", work chart for sleeve design for 4 rnds, then complete arm with gray.

Head: Work as for boy kitty.

Finishing: To make tail: Remove waste yarn from body and pick up 4 sts from top, 4 sts from bottom, and 1 st from each side of resulting hole (10 sts). With gray, work even for 4". K 2 tog around. Thread yarn through rem 5 sts, pull tightly and secure. Stuff tail and legs. Gather feet. Sew shoulders about 1" from each edge, leaving neck opening. Stuff arms and sew into armholes. Stuff body. Stuff head. Gather head about ½" from bottom edge to fit neck opening. Sew head to body. With gray yarn, sew through both thicknesses of each ear, near the outer edge, pushing stuffing toward the head.

Face: Referring to diagram, cut circles from gold, black, and pink felt for eyes and cheeks. Embroider white highlights on black circles; sew black circles to gold circles. Sew eyes and cheeks to face. With black thread, embroider nose and mouth. Cut 2 small circles of gold for buttons on boy kitty's overalls and sew in place. With black carpet thread, make whiskers and eyelashes, knotting securely.

Tie: With green, crochet a chain about 17" long. Tie in a bow around neck.

Knitting Abbreviations:
beg—begin(ning)
dpn—double-pointed needles
inc—increase
k—knit
p—purl
rem—remaining
rep—repeat
rnd(s)—round(s)
st(s)—stitch(es)
St st—stockinette stitch (k 1 row, p 1 row)
ssk—slip, slip, knit (slip sts knit-wise, k slipped sts tog)
tog—together

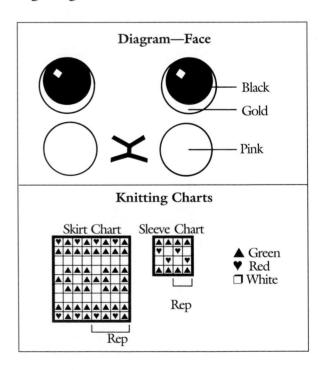

Beaded Ornaments
In Stained-Glass Colors

Give plastic canvas a stained-glass look by cross-stitching it with glass beads in dazzling colors. These ornaments are quite small—a dozen will decorate a tabletop tree.

Materials (for 12 ornaments):
charts and color key on pages 148-49
12 (3") squares of 14-count plastic canvas
#10 crewel needle
white quilting thread
beeswax
glass seed beads: 5 packages cobalt blue; 2 packages red; 1 package each green, light blue, gold
#16 Balger navy metallic braid
12 (12") pieces of ¼"-wide red ribbon (optional)

For each ornament, using doubled quilting thread, center and work design on plastic canvas according to chart. (*Note:* Wax thread with beeswax before use to prevent tangling.) Work back and forth in rows from bottom of design to top, slanting all stitches in same direction. After front of ornament is completed, turn over and work the back from same chart.

Trim canvas around each ornament, leaving 1 hole around edge for braid. Beginning at top center of round ornaments and at 1 corner of star ornaments, overcast-stitch edges of each ornament with metallic braid, leaving a 3" tail at beginning and end for hanger loop. Knot ends of braid tails.

If desired, extend hanger by threading a 12" piece of ribbon through braid loop. Tie in a bow at top of braid loop.

Woven Ribbons Make Keepsake Cookie Tins

You give two gifts when your baked goodies are packaged in these ribbon-covered tins. After the cookies have been eaten, the tins can serve as festive containers to keep other Christmas snacks fresh or to store needlework or craft supplies. This is a good way to recycle old tins or to make inexpensive new ones extraordinary. You can make the sides of the tin as fancy as you wish—use a single ribbon wide enough to cover the entire area beneath the lid, or layer several ribbons for a more elaborate effect.

Materials (for 3 tins):
charts on page 149
foam-core board
craft knife
masking tape
tweezers
washable fabric glue
heavy white paper
assorted ribbons to cover sides
    of lid and tin: ⅔ yard each for
    small and medium tins,
    1 yard each for large tin
liquid ravel preventer

For Christmas tree:
6" cookie tin with lid
9⅓ yards (⅜"-wide) green satin ribbon
9⅔ yards (⅜"-wide) gold satin ribbon

For Angel:
7¼" cookie tin with lid
6¼ yards (¼"-wide) gold satin ribbon
6¾ yards (¼"-wide) ivory satin
    ribbon

For Star:
10½" cookie tin with lid
9¾ yards (⅜"-wide) red satin ribbon
9¾ yards (⅜"-wide) gold satin
    ribbon

Number of Lengths to Cut:
Christmas Tree:
        Color A (green)—15 (8")
        Color B (gold)—16 (8")
Angel: Color A (gold)—25 (9")
        Color B (ivory)—27 (9")
Star: Color A (gold)—27 (13")
        Color B (red)—27 (13")

Trace top of cookie tin lid onto foam-core board and cut out with craft knife. For tree and star designs, draw a grid of ⅜" squares on foam-core disk. For angel, draw a grid of ¼" squares.

Beginning at vertical center of grid, lay lengths of ribbon Color A over foam-core disk, aligning ribbon with ruled lines. Secure ends of ribbons on back of foam-core with masking tape.

To weave design, referring to chart and beginning at horizontal center of grid, weave ribbon Color B through vertical ribbons. Secure ends with tape on back of foam-core. Use tweezers to lift vertical ribbons as necessary and to pull end of horizontal ribbon through. Use washable fabric glue to secure last 2 top and bottom horizontal ribbons to disk to keep them from slipping off the edge.

To secure ribbon-covered disk to tin lid, apply glue to top of lid, place disk on it, aligning edges, and weight with a heavy object until dry (15 to 20 minutes).

To finish lid, cut a strip of heavy white paper, wide enough to cover side of lid and edge of disk and long enough to wrap around lid. Glue to side of lid, covering edge of disk. This makes a smooth base for ribbon.

Using ribbon wide enough to cover side of lid, glue ribbon over paper strip, overlapping ends ¼". Apply liquid ravel preventer to ends of ribbon if necessary. Add other ribbon trim as desired.

To cover side of tin, measure depth from bottom edge of tin to ridge or indentation where bottom of lid rests. (Do not cover top edge of tin, so that lid will fit tightly.) Use 1 ribbon of this width or combine several narrower ribbons to cover side of tin. Apply glue to side of tin and glue ribbon in place, working a few inches at a time and smoothing ribbon as you go. Overlap ends of ribbon ¼", applying liquid ravel preventer to ends of ribbon if necessary.

Perfect Pines on Hearts and Squares

Here are three projects for the price of one. The same cross-stitched pine tree framed with hearts can be finished off as a simple square ornament turned on its point or, with the addition of ribbon and fabric scraps, sewn into a soft-sculpture heart. Pines and hearts alternate on the "heart pocket," a nifty little pillow that doubles as a place to store gift tags, cards, or little treasures.

ORNAMENTS

Materials (for 1 heart or 1 square ornament):
chart and pattern on pages 150-51
10" square of 28-count ivory Jobelan linen
embroidery floss (see color key)
scrap of ivory print cotton
¼ yard each (⅛"-wide) red, green, and ivory ribbon for square
¾ yard (⅜"-wide) red-and-green ribbon for heart
stuffing

Center cross-stitch design on linen and work according to chart, using 2 strands of floss. With design centered and trimming parallel to design border, trim piece to 3½" square.

Note: Pattern includes ¼" seam allowance.

For square ornament, use cross-stitched piece as a pattern and cut 1 back from ivory print. With right sides facing and raw edges aligned, stitch front to back, leaving an opening for turning. Clip corners, turn, and stuff firmly. Slipstitch opening closed.

Referring to photograph, hold 2 (6") pieces of ⅛" ribbon together as 1 and form a loop. Tack ends to top corner of square for hanger. Holding 3 (8") pieces of ⅛" ribbon together as 1, tie a bow and tack to top front of ornament.

For heart ornament, make front by transferring heart top pattern to ivory print and cut 2. With right sides facing and raw edges aligned, stitch straight edge of 1 heart top to 1 side of design piece top. Repeat for other side. Press seams toward heart top. Cut 2 (3½") pieces of ⅜" ribbon. Topstitch 1 piece of ribbon to heart over each seam line (see photograph).

For heart back, use heart front as a pattern and cut 1 from ivory print. With right sides facing and raw edges aligned, stitch heart front to back, leaving an opening for turning. Clip curves, turn, and stuff firmly. Slipstitch opening closed.

Form a loop with a 6" length of ⅜" ribbon and tack ends to top of heart for hanger. Tie a bow with remaining ribbon and tack to top front of heart.

PINE TREE HEART POCKET

Materials:
chart and patterns on pages 150-51
1 (11½" x 15") piece of 18-count ivory
    Aida cloth
embroidery floss (see color key)
¼ yard (45"-wide) red Christmas
    print
scrap of green Christmas print
9" piece of green piping to match
    Christmas print
30" piece of 1"-wide pregathered ivory
    eyelet
2 (12") pieces of ⅜"-wide Christmas
    ribbon
stuffing
1 yard (⅛"-wide) red ribbon
½ yard (¼"-wide) ivory
    ribbon

Center and work cross-stitch design on Aida
cloth according to chart, using 2 strands of
floss.
  Note: Pattern includes ¼" seam allowance.

Center pocket pattern on cross-stitched piece,
leaving ½" of unstitched fabric above top row of
trees. Cut 1. Transfer patterns to fabrics and cut
out. With right sides facing and raw edges
aligned, baste piping to top edge of cross-stitched
piece. With right sides facing and raw edges
aligned, stitch cross-stitched pocket to lining
along top edge only. Turn and press.

With right sides up and raw edges aligned,
position pocket on red print heart and baste in
place. With raw edges aligned, baste pregathered
lace around heart front. For hanger, with raw
edges aligned, pin 1 end of each 12" piece of
ribbon to right side of heart pocket as indicated
on pattern. With right sides facing and raw edges
aligned and keeping remaining ribbon ends free,
stitch heart front to green heart back, leaving an
opening for turning. Clip curves, turn, and stuff.
Slipstitch opening closed.

From ⅛"-wide red ribbon, cut 4 (9") pieces.
Cut ivory ribbon in half. Holding 2 pieces of red
ribbon and 1 piece of ivory ribbon as 1, tie in a
bow and tack to 1 side of heart top (see
photograph). Repeat for other side. For hanger,
tie Christmas ribbon ends together.

Crochet a Stocking And Tree Skirt

This crocheted stocking is big enough to hold plenty of goodies, and the matching skirt makes an attractive base for piles of presents. Each piece is stitched in long single crochet from top to bottom (instead of side to side), which gives it a dense texture.

Materials:
worsted-weight wool (220-yd.,
    100-gr. skein): 2 skeins cream,
    1 skein each green, red (for stocking);
    4 skeins cream, 2 skeins green, 1 skein
    red (for tree skirt)
size H crochet hook (or size to obtain
    gauge)
stitch markers

GENERAL INSTRUCTIONS

Finished Size: Stocking is about 23" long. Tree skirt is about 35" in diameter.

Gauge: 10 sts and 16 rows = 3" in main pat. 10 sts and 9 rows = 3" in plaid pat.

Long dc for plaid pat: Yo and insert hook in st 1 row below, yo and pull up a lp to height of current row, complete st as a dc working over and around ch-3 lp.

Main pat: Pat is worked over an odd number of sts; add 1 for base ch. *Row 1* (right side): Sc in 2nd ch from hook and ea ch across. Turn. *Row 2:* Ch 1 for first sc, * insert hook in st 1 row below next st, pull up a lp to height of current row, yo and pull through all lps on hook (long sc made), sc in next st, rep from * across. Turn. *Row 3* (right side): Ch 1 for first sc, * sc in next st, long sc in next st, rep from * across to last 2 sts, sc in ea of last 2 sts. Rep rows 2 and 3 for main pat.

Holly leaf: With green, ch 13. Sc in 3rd ch from hook, (dc in ea of next 2 sts, ch 2, sl st in bump on back of 2nd ch from hook, dc in next st, sc in ea of next 2 sts) twice, ch 3, working along opposite side of base ch, sc in same st as last sc, (sc in next st, dc in next st, ch 2, sl st in bump on back of 2nd ch from hook, dc in ea of next 2 sts, sc in next st) twice, sl st in next st. Fasten off.

Berry: With red, ch 4, join with a sl st to form a ring. *Rnd 1:* Ch 1, work 6 sc in ring. *Rnd 2:* Ch 1, sc in ea of next 6 sc, sl st in first sc. Gather ends of tube to make berry.

STOCKING

With green, ch 50. *Row 1:* Sc in 2nd ch from hook and ea ch across. Turn. *Row 2:* Ch 1 for first sc, sc in ea sc across = 49 sts (including beg ch-1). Turn. *Row 3* (beg plaid pat): Ch 3 for first dc, dc in next st, * ch 3, sk 3 sc, dc in ea of next 3 sts, rep from * across, end with ch 3, sk 3 sc, dc in ea of next 2 sc. Fasten off. Turn. *Row 4:* Join cream, ch 3 for first dc, sk 1 st, * work 3 long dc as specified above, ch 3, sk 3 sts, rep from * across, end with 3 long dc, ch 3, sl st in last st. Fasten off. Turn. *Row 5:* Join red, ch 3 for first dc, long dc in next st, * ch 3, sk 3 sts, 3 long dc, rep from * across, end with ch 3, sk 3 sts, long dc in ea of last 2 sts. Fasten off. Turn. *Rows 6-14:* Rep rows 4 and 5 alternately, working 1 row ea with green, cream, and red for plaid pat. *Row 15* (end plaid pat): Join green, ch 3 for first dc, long dc in next st, * sc in ea of next 3 dc, work 3 long dc, rep from * across, end with sc in ea of next 3 dc, long dc in ea of last 2 sts. Turn. *Row 16:* Ch 1 for first sc, sc in ea st across. Fasten off. Turn. *Row 17* (right side): Join cream, ch 1 for first sc, sc in ea st across. Turn. *Row 18 and following rows:* Rep rows 2 and 3 of main pat until piece measures 14" from beg, ending after a wrong side row. Fasten off.

Heel opening: With right side facing and cream, ch 12, sk 12 sts on stocking, join yarn in next st and work in main pat across next 25 sts, ch 13, leave last 12 sts unworked, turn. Sc in 2nd ch from hook and ea of next 11 ch, work in main pat across 25 sts, sc in ea of 12 ch. Turn. Ch 1 for first sc, work across next 10 sts in main pat, pull up a lp in ea of next 3 sts, yo and through all lps on hook (dec over 3 sts made), work across next 21 sts in main pat, dec over next 3 sts, work across rem 11 sts in main pat = 45 sts across.

Turn. Ch 1 for first sc, work even in main pat for 3 rows. Ch 1 for first sc, working in main pat, work next 10 sts, dec over next 3 sts, work 17 sts, dec over next 3 sts, work 11 sts = 41 sts across. Work even in main pat until piece measures 5½" from heel opening, ending after a wrong side row. Fasten off. Turn.

Toe: Rows 1 and 2: Join green, ch 1 for first sc, sc in ea st across. Turn. *Row 3:* Ch 1 for first sc, sc in ea of next 7 sts, dec over next 2 sts, sc in next st, place a marker on sc just made, dec over next 2 sts, sc in ea of next 15 sts, dec over next 2 sts, sc in next st, place a marker on sc just made, dec over next 2 sts, sc in ea of 8 sts = 37 sts across. Turn. *Row 4:* Ch 1 for first sc, sc in ea st across. Turn. *Rows 5-11:* Ch 1 for first sc, * sc in ea st to 2 sts before marker, dec over next 2 sts, sc in marker st, dec over next 2 sts, rep from * across, end with sc in ea rem st. Turn. *Row 12:* Do not ch 1, sk first st, dec over next 2 sts, dec over next 3 sts, dec over next 2 sts, sl st in last st. Fasten off.

Heel: Row 1: With right side facing, join green in st at edge of heel opening, sc in ea of next 12 sts, sc in corner of opening, place a marker on sc just made, sc in ea of next 12 sts. Turn. *Row 2:* Ch 1 for first sc, sc in ea st across to 2 sts before marker, dec over next 2 sts, sc in marker st, dec over next 2 sts, sc in ea rem st. Turn. Rep row 2 until only 5 sts rem. *Last row:* Do not ch 1, sk first st, dec over next 3 sts, sl st in last st. Fasten off. Work other side of heel in same manner.

Finishing: Sew stocking seam. Join green to top of stocking in st at seam and sl st in ea st around opening, end with sl st in first sl st. Ch 11, sl st in 2nd ch from hook and ea rem ch. Fasten off. To make hanger, tack end of ch-11 to base of ch.

Make 2 holly leaves and 3 berries. Tack to stocking (see photograph).

TREE SKIRT

Row 1: With green, ch 72, sc in 2nd ch from hook and ea ch across = 71 sc. Turn. *Rows 2 and 3:* Ch 1 for first sc, sc in ea st across. Turn. Fasten off. *Row 4:* Join cream and work row 2 of main pat. Turn. *Row 5* (right side): Work row

3 of main pat. Turn. *First inc row:* Ch 1 for first sc, (long sc in next st, sc in next st) twice, * 3 long sc in next st, (sc in next st, long sc in next st) 5 times, sc in next st, rep from * 4 times more, 3 long sc in next st, sc in next st, (long sc in next st, sc in next st) twice, turn. Mark the center st of ea 3-long-sc corner grp with stitch markers. Remember to move markers up ea row. *2nd inc row:* Ch 1 for first sc, work across in main pat, except work 1 sc in ea st of corner grp, turn. *3rd inc row:* Ch 1 for first sc, * long sc in next st, sc in next st, rep from * across, turn. *4th inc row:* Ch 1 for first sc, work across in main pat, except work 3 long sc in marked st. Continue with cream in main pat and rep 2nd, 3rd, and 4th inc rows until there are 45 sts bet marked sts. Fasten off. Turn. *Next row:* Join green, (ch 1 for first sc, sc in ea st across, turn) twice.

Beg plaid pat: Row 1: With green, ch 3 for first dc, * dc in each of next 3 sts, (ch 3, sk 3 sts, dc in ea of next 3 sts) across to marked st, ch 3, sk marked st, rep from * across, end with dc in last st. Fasten off. Turn. *Row 2:* Join red and ch 4, sk 3 sts, * (3 long dc, ch 3, sk 3 sts) across to marked st, work 3 long dc over ch-3 and into corner (skipped) st of row below, ch 3, sk 3 sts, rep from * across, end with sl st in last st. Fasten off. Turn. *Row 3:* Join cream, ch 3 for first dc, * 3 long dc, (ch 3, sk 3 sts, 3 long dc) to corner grp, ch 1, work 3 long dc in center st of red grp, ch 1, rep from * across, end with long dc in last st. Fasten off. Turn. *Row 4:* Join green and ch 4, sk 3 sts, * (3 long dc, ch 3, sk 3 sts) to corner grp, work 3 long dc over ch-1 and into first st of red grp below, ch 1, work 3 long dc over ch-1 and into last st of red grp, ch 3, sk 3 sts, rep from * across, end with sl st in last st. Fasten off. Turn. *Row 5:* Join red, ch 3 for first dc, * (3 long dc, ch 3, sk 3 sts) to corner grp, work 3 long dc over ch-1 and into center st of cream grp below, ch 3, sk 3 sts, rep from * across, end with long dc in last st. Fasten off. Turn. *Row 6:* Join cream and ch 4, sk 3 sts, * 3 long dc, (ch 3, sk 3 sts, 3 long dc) to corner grp, ch 1, sk first st of red grp, 3 dc in center st of red grp, ch 1, sk last st of red grp, rep from * across, end with sl st in last st. Fasten off. Turn. *Row 7:* Join green, ch 3 for first dc, * (3 long dc, ch 3, sk 3 sts) to corner grp, 3 long dc over ch-1 and into first st of red grp below, ch 1,

work 3 long dc in last st of red grp below, ch 3, sk 3 sts, rep from * across, end with long dc in last st. Fasten off. Turn. *Row 8:* Join red and ch 4, sk 3 sts, * (3 long dc, ch 3, sk 3 sts) across to corner grp, work 3 long dc over ch-1 and into center st of cream grp below, ch 3, sk 3 sts, rep from * across, end with long dc in last st. Fasten off. Turn. *Rows 9-12:* Rep rows 3-6 of plaid pat following established color sequence. *Row 13:* Join green, ch 3 for first dc, * (3 long dc, sc in ea of next 3 sts) to corner grp, 3 long dc over ch-1 and into first st of red grp below, sc in ea st of cream grp, 3 long dc over ch-1 into 3rd st of red grp below, sc in ea of 3 sts, rep from * across, end with long dc in last st. Turn. (Ch 1 for first sc, sc in ea st across, turn) twice. Fasten off.

Edging: With right side facing, join green in corner and work 53 sc along 1 edge of skirt opening, turn. (Ch 1 for first sc, sc in ea st across, turn) twice. Fasten off. Rep edging across rem edge of skirt opening. Do not fasten off or turn. Ch 1, sl st in ea st around entire skirt. Fasten off.

Finishing: Make 12 holly leaves and 18 berries. Tack 2 holly leaves and 3 berries to skirt at each corner point on main pat (see photograph). Make 8 ties as follows: Ch 40 with green and work a sl st in ea ch across. Fasten off. Tack ties along edges of skirt opening.

Crochet Abbreviations
beg—begin(ning)
bet—between
ch—chain(s)
dc—double crochet
dec—decrease(s)
ea—each
grp—group
inc—increase(s)
lp(s)—loop(s)
pat—pattern
rep—repeat
rem—remain(ing)
rnd—round
sc—single crochet
sk—skip
sl st—slip stitch
st(s)—stitch(es)
yo—yarn over

Smiling Eskimos for Earmuffs and Sweater

Perk up a sweater or a sweatshirt with felt-and-fur appliqués. For the matching earmuffs, just stitch fur and felt to purchased frames for an original, hand-crafted accessory.

ESKIMO SWEATER

Materials:
patterns on page 153
scraps of felt: light blue, lavender, purple, cobalt blue, black, flesh
compass
embroidery scissors
scraps of white fake fur
embroidery floss: light blue, rose, hot pink, dark blue, lavender, white
1 red sweater, cardigan, or sweatshirt, any size
washable fabric glue
craft stick
silver Balger blending filament
thread to match fabrics

Note: To cut fur, use embroidery scissors and cut from the back of fur. Keep blades of scissors close to backing and make small cuts. Handwash completed garment in cold water. Lay flat to dry.

Transfer patterns for clothing and boots to felt and cut out. Transfer patterns for muff and mittens to fur and cut out. From fur, cut 3 (2"-diameter) circles for hats. For girl, center and cut ½"-diameter circle from center of 1 circle. Center and cut ⅝" circles from centers of remaining fur circles. Referring to photograph and patterns, embroider details on clothing.

From flesh-colored felt, cut 3 (1"-diameter) circles for faces. Using face pattern for earmuffs as a guide, center and embroider faces on Eskimos, omitting cheeks. Center 1 face piece behind each fur piece and slipstitch felt to fur.

Position Eskimos on front of garment as desired, starting with boots, then clothing, and then hats and muff or mittens. Using craft stick, apply glue to back of each pattern piece; then gently press piece onto garment. Let dry.

Using 1 strand of blending filament and 2 strands of white floss, randomly embroider stars (cross-stitch over straightstitch) on front of garment.

ESKIMO EARMUFFS

Materials:
pattern on page 153
10" square of white fake fur
compass
embroidery scissors
scraps of flesh-colored felt
embroidery floss: light blue, rose, hot pink
threads to match fabrics
2 (6⅛"-long) pieces of ⅜"-wide elastic
1 pair of earmuff frames (see Resources, page 156)
stuffing

Note: To cut fur, use embroidery scissors and cut from the back of fur. Keep blades of scissors close to backing and make small cuts.

From fur, cut 2 (4½"-diameter) circles and 2 (3½"-diameter) circles. Center and cut 1 (1½"-diameter) circle from center of each 4½" fur circle. Transfer face pattern to flesh-colored felt and cut 2. Embroider features as indicated. Center 1 face behind each 4½" fur piece and slipstitch face to fur.

To fit face piece to earmuff frame, stitch 1 piece of elastic around edge of fur on wrong side of 1 face piece, pulling elastic tightly to gather while stitching. Continue around circle until ends meet. Fur will be slightly puckered.

Position face piece on outside of earmuff frame over metal circle. With face centered and top of face piece toward headband, baste face piece to frame.

To finish, place small amount of stuffing inside face piece for padding. Position 1 (3½"-diameter) fur circle over padding and slipstitch to face piece. Repeat for other face piece.

Punched-Paper Card Sends
A Lacy Greeting

Wish your friends a peace-filled Christmas with this lacy angel card. It's easy to make—you just punch holes in the paper with pins of various sizes. Gold foil shows through the pinholes to give the effect of showers of stardust. Use purchased envelopes to mail the cards—you should be able to find ones large enough for 5-inch by 7-inch cards at a stationer's or quick-copy print shop.

Materials:
pattern on page 152
tracing paper
11" x 8" piece of white watercolor paper
½"-thick piece of craft foam
pins or thumb tacks
3 different sizes of pins, such as diaper pin, straight pin, and thumb tack
gold foil paper
craft knife
hole punch
craft glue

Transfer pattern to tracing paper. Fold white paper in half to mark center. Open and place on craft foam. Lay pattern over card front, centering design and aligning left edge with center fold of card. Secure pattern and paper with pins or thumb tacks.

Make angel outline by pushing pin with largest diameter through pattern and card into craft foam. Make eye with large pin. For face, use medium-sized pin and use smallest pin for feathers in wings, dress details, and strands of hair. For rays of light radiating from star, use largest pin close to star and gradually mix in holes from small pin. Make outer ends of rays with small pin.

Cut out star using craft knife. Remove pattern and card from craft foam. Fold card and trim to 5" x 7".

Transfer building shapes to gold foil paper and cut out, using hole punch to make round window. Referring to pattern, position and glue building shapes to bottom front of card. Cut a piece of gold paper to 5" x 7" and attach to inside front of card with double-sided tape so that gold paper shows through holes and star.

Cinnamon Angels for Your Tree

So many of us become traditionalists at Christmas—a wreath on the door, a beautiful tree in the great room, and the scent of cinnamon in the air. Bring this old-fashioned aroma to your home with cinnamon-dough ornaments. The recipe here is an old family one from craftswoman Sylvia Pinnow of Delaware. She says that the secret to success is to use the best quality of cinnamon you can find.

Materials (for 8 angels):
pattern below
tracing paper
1 cup of cinnamon
¼ cup of wood glue
¾ cup of warm water
1 small bottle of cinnamon oil
cinnamon to dust work surface
plastic drinking straw
toothpick
2 yards (⅛"-wide) red satin ribbon

Transfer pattern to paper and cut out. Put cinnamon in mixing bowl. In a separate container, combine glue with warm water and add to cinnamon. Mix. Dough will be stiff. Add cinnamon oil.

Dust work surface with cinnamon. Turn out dough and knead. Dough will be stiff at first but will become elastic. Let dough rest 15 minutes.

Knead again. If dough crumbles, add warm water 1 teaspoon at a time.

Roll dough ¼" thick. Lay pattern on dough; using a knife, trim around pattern. Cut a 1" piece of drinking straw and insert in top of ornament to make a hole for hanging. Leave straw in place until ornament dries.

Using toothpick, make eyes and other features. Use a series of deep dots to create lines so as not to stretch ornament.

Allow ornament to dry naturally. Turn twice daily to prevent curling. Ornament will shrink to ¾ of original size. For hanger, cut 9" piece of ribbon. Thread ribbon through hole and knot ends together.

Pattern is full-size.

Cut pattern from dough along heavy black lines.

97

Don Sequins and Beads For the Holidays

Whether you're attending a Christmas tea or the office party, go in style in clothing you've embellished yourself. Party shoes and matching sweaters that glitter with sequins, jewels, and beading can be expensive to buy, but you can make your own for a fraction of the cost. We decorated the sweater on the left simply by stitching a beaded fleur-de-lis appliqué to the front and adding a strip of beaded braid to the cuff. Look for similar beaded appliqués in the wedding and formal wear section of a fabric store or order them from craft supply catalogs.

If you plan to remove the appliqué after the holidays, simply tack it in place, using thread that blends with the background of the appliqué. If you want to make it a permanent embellishment, check to be sure that the appliqué is hand washable.

For the matching shoes, we glued black-and-gold beaded bows to inexpensive velveteen flats, using a craft glue recommended for use on fabrics.

Sweaters encrusted with sequins and beading, like those you see in stores, require more time and skill than most of us can manage. But for a quick-and-easy sequined sweater, buy about a yard each of several widths and colors of sequin trims. (We used a double-strand serpentine trim, one in red and one in green, and a wider trim in gold for the sweater shown on the right.) Experiment with arranging the trims on the sweater until you find a design you like. It's a good idea to try the sweater on with the trims pinned or taped in place so that you can see how they will lie. Pin each trim in place and use matching thread to baste it to the sweater. Then stitch on acrylic jewels, pearls, mirrors, or whatever else your imagination suggests.

To make the matching shoes, we glued two sizes of star-shaped acrylic jewels and a yard of single-strand sequins onto velveteen flats. You can secure the jewels by using a low-melt hot-glue gun. It's best to attach the sequin trim by tracing the design onto the shoe with fabric glue and then pressing the trim carefully and firmly in place. Remember that the trim is fragile, so you won't want to click your heels when you wear these magic slippers.

Celebrations
from
the Kitchen

Cookies Kids Love

Holidays take on a special magic when viewed through the eyes of children. Sugar plums, twinkling lights, and Santa on the street corner are all part of a child's Christmas. So too is the tradition of baking Christmas cookies with family members. And these cookies definitely capture the fantasy of childhood. The pudgy chocolate bear and peanut buttery mice are adorable and are easy enough for little hands to shape. Children will love rolling dough balls and then flattening them to form the bear. And what fun it will be for them to accent the mice with peanut ears and a licorice tail! The

Teddy Bear Cookies recipe will make 12 fat little bears, and the Christmas Mice Cookies recipe will make 48 enchanting little mice.

TEDDY BEAR COOKIES

½ cup butter or margarine,
   softened
1 cup sugar
2 large eggs
2 (1-ounce) squares unsweetened
   chocolate, melted
2 teaspoons vanilla extract
2 cups all-purpose flour
½ teaspoon baking soda
½ teaspoon salt
1 (4.25-ounce) tube red decorator
   frosting
1 (4.25-ounce) tube white decorator
   frosting

Beat butter at medium speed with an electric mixer until fluffy; gradually add sugar, beating well. Add eggs, one at a time, beating after each addition. Stir in melted chocolate and vanilla.

Combine flour, soda, and salt; gradually add to creamed mixture, mixing well. Cover and chill 2 hours.

Divide dough into 12 balls. Cut one ball in half. For bear's body, shape one half into a ball; place on an ungreased cookie sheet, and flatten into a 3- x 2½-inch oval. Cut remaining half into 2 equal portions. For bear's head, shape one portion into a round ball, and flatten on cookie sheet, slightly overlapping body.

Pinch off a small piece from remaining portion for nose; position on head. Roll remaining dough into a 5-inch-long rope. Cut two ½-inch pieces for ears and four 1-inch pieces for legs. Roll each piece into a ball. Attach ears and legs to bear's body; flatten slightly. Repeat with remaining balls of dough.

Bake at 350° for 10 minutes or until cookies are almost set. Cool on cookie sheets on wire racks. Remove from pan when completely cooled. Decorate with frosting. Yield: 12 cookies.

Tips: When baking several batches of cookies, let cookie sheets cool before reusing. Most unbaked cookies can be frozen up to one year; most baked cookies freeze up to six months.

CHRISTMAS MICE COOKIES

½ cup margarine, softened
1 cup creamy peanut butter
½ cup firmly packed brown sugar
½ cup sugar
1 large egg
1 teaspoon vanilla extract
1½ cups all-purpose flour
½ teaspoon baking soda
   Peanuts
1 (2.25-ounce) jar red cinnamon
   candies
4 yards of thin red licorice, cut into
   3-inch pieces

Beat margarine and peanut butter at medium speed with an electric mixer; gradually add sugars, beating well. Add egg and vanilla; beat well.

Combine flour and soda; gradually add to creamed mixture, mixing well. Cover and chill at least 2 hours.

Shape dough into 1-inch balls; taper one end of each ball to form a tear-drop shape. Press one side flat; place flat sides on ungreased cookie sheets with cookies 2 inches apart. Press in sides of dough to raise backs of mice. Gently place 2 peanut halves in dough for ears. With a wooden pick, make a ½-inch-deep hole at tail end.

Bake at 350° for 9 minutes; remove cookies from oven. Place red cinnamon candies in cookies for eyes; bake an additional 1 to 2 minutes or until browned. Remove from oven; insert licorice tails and cool completely on baking sheets. Yield: 4 dozen.

Sweet Dreams, Chocolate Fantasies

Sinfully rich, but worth every calorie, these desserts are a chocolate lover's delight—any of them would be a delicious finale for your holiday entertaining.

CHOCOLATE-RASPBERRY ROULAGE

½ cup sifted cake flour
3 tablespoons cocoa
¾ teaspoon baking powder
3 large eggs, separated
½ cup sugar, divided
2 tablespoons milk
⅛ teaspoon salt
1 to 2 tablespoons powdered sugar
1 cup whipping cream
3 tablespoons powdered sugar
1 teaspoon vanilla extract
1 (10-ounce) jar seedless red raspberry
   jam, divided
   Sifted powdered sugar
   Raspberry Sauce
   Garnishes: powdered sugar, fresh
   mint, fresh raspberries, whipping
   cream

Chocolate at its very best: pictured here are Chocolate Raspberry Roulage and Cream-Filled Chocolate Cake.

Grease bottom and sides of a 15- x 10- x 1-inch jellyroll pan; line with wax paper, and grease paper. Set aside.

Combine flour, cocoa, and baking powder; set aside.

Beat egg yolks at high speed with an electric mixer until foamy. Gradually add ¼ cup sugar, beating until thick and lemon colored (about 5 minutes). Add milk; stir in flour mixture.

Beat egg whites and salt until foamy; gradually add remaining ¼ cup sugar, beating until soft peaks form. Fold into batter; spread evenly into prepared pan. Bake at 375° for 10 to 12 minutes.

Sift 1 to 2 tablespoons powdered sugar in a 15- x 10-inch rectangle on a towel. When cake is done, immediately loosen from sides of pan, and turn out onto sugared towel. Peel off wax paper. Starting at narrow end, roll up cake and towel together; let cool completely on a wire rack, seam side down.

Beat whipping cream until foamy; gradually add 3 tablespoons powdered sugar and vanilla, beating until soft peaks form. Unroll cake. Reserve 2 tablespoons raspberry jam for Raspberry Sauce; spread remaining jam on cake. Carefully spread whipped cream mixture over jam.

Reroll cake, without towel, and place on serving plate, seam side down. Sprinkle with powdered

sugar. To serve, place cake slice on top of Raspberry Sauce. Garnish, if desired. Yield: 8 to 10 servings.

Raspberry Sauce:

- 2 (10-ounce) packages frozen red raspberries, thawed
- 2 tablespoons cornstarch
- 2 tablespoons reserved seedless red raspberry jam
- ½ teaspoon almond extract

Place raspberries in container of an electric blender; process until smooth. Strain and discard seeds.

Combine cornstarch and remaining ingredients in a small saucepan, stirring until cornstarch dissolves; stir in raspberry puree. Cook over medium heat, stirring constantly, until mixture comes to a boil. Let boil 1 minute, stirring constantly. Remove from heat. Cover and chill. Yield: 1¼ cups.

CREAM-FILLED CHOCOLATE CAKE

- ¾ cup cocoa
- 1 cup boiling water
- 2 tablespoons butter or margarine, softened
- 2 cups sugar
- 2 cups sifted cake flour
- 1 teaspoon baking soda
- ½ teaspoon baking powder
- 1 teaspoon salt
- ½ cup shortening
- ½ cup buttermilk
- 2 large eggs
- 1 teaspoon vanilla extract
  Cream Filling
  Chocolate Frosting
  Garnish: Chocolate Bow

Grease bottoms and sides of three 8-inch round cakepans; line with wax paper, and grease paper. Set aside. Combine first 3 ingredients, stirring until mixture is smooth; set aside.

Combine sugar and next 4 ingredients in a large mixing bowl; add cocoa mixture and shortening, beating at medium speed with an electric mixer until blended. Add buttermilk, eggs, and vanilla; beat 2 minutes or until blended. Pour batter into prepared pans. Bake at 350° for 20 to 25 minutes or until a wooden pick inserted in center comes out clean. Cool in pans on wire racks 10 minutes; remove layers from pans. Remove wax paper, and let cool completely on wire racks.

Spread Cream Filling between layers. Spread Chocolate Frosting on top and sides of cake. Garnish, if desired. Yield: one 3-layer cake.

Cream Filling:

- 2 tablespoons all-purpose flour
- ¼ cup milk
- ¼ cup shortening
- 2 tablespoons butter or margarine, softened
- 2 teaspoons vanilla extract
- ⅛ teaspoon salt
- 2 cups sifted powdered sugar

Combine flour and milk in a small saucepan; cook over low heat, stirring constantly with a wire whisk, until mixture begins to thicken. Remove from heat; cool. Cover and chill at least 1 hour.

Beat shortening and butter at low speed with an electric mixer. Add chilled flour mixture, vanilla, and salt; beat until smooth. Gradually add powdered sugar; beat at high speed 4 to 5 minutes or until light and fluffy. Yield: 1¼ cups.

Chocolate Frosting:

- ½ cup butter or margarine, softened
- 3 (1-ounce) squares unsweetened chocolate, melted
- ⅓ cup milk
- 2 teaspoons vanilla extract
- 1 (16-ounce) package powdered sugar, sifted

Beat butter and chocolate at low speed with an electric mixer until smooth. Blend in milk and vanilla extract. Gradually add powdered sugar; beat at high speed 5 minutes or until fluffy. Yield: 2½ cups.

Above: Give a cake a spectacular flourish with this frilly chocolate bow. Here spectacular is easy. Form the bow by using soft chocolate strips that have been cut with a pastry wheel.

CHOCOLATE BOW

    6 (1-ounce) squares semisweet
         chocolate
    3½ tablespoons light corn syrup

Melt chocolate in a small saucepan over low heat; stir in corn syrup. Cover and refrigerate 1 hour.

Knead chocolate until it is consistency of dough. (Kneading with warm hands keeps chocolate soft; letting it stand on a cool surface hardens it.) Roll out onto a cool surface to ⅛-inch thickness. Using a fluted pastry wheel, cut into seven 8- to 10-inch strips (about ¼ inch wide). Place ends of 5 strips together to form loops. Turn a 9-inch round cakepan upside down; arrange loops to form a bow; loosely attach remaining 2 strips for ribbon. Let stand 8 hours. Carefully remove pieces, and arrange on top of cake. Yield: one bow.

Note: Dough may be wrapped and stored at room temperature up to 1 month.

CHOCOLATE PARADISE PIE

    3 large eggs, separated
    1 cup sugar
    ½ cup chopped pecans
   10 saltine crackers, crushed
    1 cup semisweet chocolate morsels
    1 tablespoon Kahlúa or other
         coffee-flavored liqueur
         Dash of salt
    ¾ cup milk
    1 cup whipping cream, whipped
         Garnish: chocolate curls or
           shavings

Beat egg whites at high speed with an electric mixer until foamy. Gradually add sugar, beating until stiff peaks form. Fold in pecans and cracker crumbs.

Spoon meringue into a well-greased 9-inch pieplate. Using the back of a spoon, shape meringue into a pie shell. Bake at 300° for 40 minutes. Cool on a wire rack.

Combine chocolate morsels, Kahlúa, and salt in container of an electric blender; set aside.

Combine milk and egg yolks in a heavy saucepan. Cook over medium heat, stirring constantly, until mixture begins to boil; remove from heat. (Mixture may look curdled.) Pour into blender; process until smooth. Pour chocolate mixture into cooled meringue shell; cover loosely and chill until firm.

Spread whipped cream over filling; garnish, if desired. Yield: one 9-inch pie.

CHOCOLATE-CANDY CHEESECAKE

    1 (9-ounce) package chocolate wafer
         cookies, crushed
    ¼ cup sugar
    ¼ cup butter or margarine, melted
    2 (2.07-ounce) chocolate-coated
         caramel-peanut nougat bars,
         coarsely chopped
    2 (8-ounce) packages cream cheese,
         softened
    ½ cup sugar
    2 large eggs
    ¾ cup semisweet chocolate morsels,
         melted
    1 teaspoon vanilla extract
         Whipped cream

Combine first 3 ingredients; press mixture evenly onto bottom and 1½ inches up sides of a 9-inch springform pan. Sprinkle chopped nougat bars evenly over bottom; set aside.

Beat cream cheese at high speed with an electric mixer until light and fluffy; gradually add ½ cup sugar, mixing well. Add eggs, one at a time, beating after each addition. Stir in chocolate morsels and vanilla; beat until blended. Spoon over candy layer. Bake at 350° for 30 minutes. Remove from oven, and run a knife around edge of pan to release sides. Let cool to room temperature on a wire rack. Cover and chill at least 8 hours.

To serve, remove cheesecake from pan; pipe or dollop whipped cream on top. Yield: one 9-inch cheesecake.

CHOCOLATE-MINT SOUFFLE

　　1　envelope unflavored gelatin
　¼　cup water
　　3　large eggs, lightly beaten
　½　cup sugar
　½　cup milk
　½　cup semisweet chocolate
　　　morsels
　½　teaspoon peppermint extract
1½　cups whipping cream, whipped
　　　Crème Fraîche Sauce
　　　Chocolate Pastries

Sprinkle gelatin over water in a medium saucepan; let stand 1 minute. Add eggs, sugar, and milk; cook over medium heat, stirring constantly, until mixture begins to boil. Remove from heat; stir in chocolate morsels and peppermint extract. Cool. Fold in whipped cream; spoon into individual serving dishes. Cover and chill. Just before serving, dollop Crème Fraîche Sauce on soufflé and insert 2 pastries. Yield: 6 servings.

Crème Fraîche Sauce:

　½　cup whipping cream
2½　tablespoons sifted powdered
　　　sugar
　2　tablespoons sour cream
　¼　teaspoon vanilla extract

Combine all ingredients in a small bowl; beat at high speed with an electric mixer until soft peaks form. Yield: 1¼ cups.

Chocolate Pastries:

　1　(9-inch) refrigerated piecrust
　1　(2-ounce) square chocolate-flavored
　　　candy coating, melted

Roll pastry on a lightly floured surface. Cut into desired shape using a 2-inch cookie cutter, and place on a lightly greased baking sheet. Bake at 400° for 6 minutes or until lightly browned. Remove from baking sheet and cool on wire racks. Drizzle with melted coating. Store in an airtight container. Yield: 12 pastries.

CHOCOLATE TIRAMISU

　　4　egg yolks
　　1　cup sugar
　¼　cup whipping cream
　　1　(8-ounce) package cream cheese,
　　　　softened
2½　tablespoons sour cream
　⅓　cup cocoa
　　2　tablespoons Kahlúa or other
　　　　coffee-flavored liqueur
　⅔　cup whipping cream
　　2　(3-ounce) packages ladyfingers
1¼　cups whipping cream
　　3　tablespoons powdered sugar
　　　　Garnish: chocolate shavings

Combine first 3 ingredients in top of a double boiler; beat at medium speed with an electric mixer until thick and pale. Bring water to a boil; reduce heat to low, and cook, stirring constantly, 8 to 10 minutes or until mixture reaches 160°. Remove from heat; cool to room temperature.

Combine cream cheese and sour cream in a large bowl; beat at medium speed until smooth. Add custard mixture, cocoa, and Kahlúa, beating until smooth.

Beat ⅔ cup whipping cream in small bowl until soft peaks form; fold into cream cheese mixture.

Line bottom and sides of a 9- x 5- x 3-inch loafpan with wax paper. Split ladyfingers in half lengthwise; line bottom and sides of pan with ladyfingers, and pour in half of cream cheese mixture. Layer ladyfingers on top; cover with remaining cream cheese mixture. Arrange remaining ladyfingers on top; cover and chill 8 hours. Unmold onto serving tray.

Beat 1¼ cups whipping cream until foamy; gradually add powdered sugar, beating until soft peaks form. Pipe or dollop whipped cream around bottom and on top. Garnish, if desired. Yield: 8 servings.

Tip: Make chocolate shavings by pulling a vegetable peeler across the surface of a square of semisweet chocolate.

Above: Brownie Trifle is the ultimate sweet extravaganza. Sample your way through each of the chocolate layers, to experience a variety of textures and flavors.

BROWNIE TRIFLE

1 (19.8-ounce) package fudge brownie mix
¼ cup praline or coffee-flavored liqueur (optional)
1 (3.5-ounce) package instant chocolate mousse mix
8 (1.4-ounce) toffee-flavored candy bars, crushed
1 (12-ounce) container frozen whipped topping, thawed
Garnish: chocolate curls

Prepare brownie mix and bake according to package directions in a 13- x 9- x 2-inch pan. Prick top of warm brownies at 1-inch intervals using a meat fork, and brush with liqueur, if desired. Let cool, and crumble.

Prepare chocolate mousse according to package directions, omitting chilling.

Place half of crumbled brownies in bottom of a 3-quart trifle dish. Top with half of mousse, crushed candy bars, and whipped topping. Repeat layers with remaining ingredients, ending with whipped topping. Garnish, if desired. Chill 8 hours. Yield: 16 to 18 servings.

107

When arranging a buffet table, the most important consideration should be traffic flow. Placement of the food should allow for easy circulation around the table. Beverages can be placed on a side table.

A Cocktail Buffet Makes Entertaining Easy

Delectable dishes and a pleasing social setting are key elements to a successful party. However, during the busy days of Christmas, the elements of ease and practicality are equally important. A cocktail buffet is oftentimes an ideal party choice. This type of gathering will accommodate many people without great expense. Furthermore, with the menu featured here, many of the dishes can be prepared ahead of time or bought commercially and simply arranged—all of which helps make party planning less hectic. Now those final moments before guests arrive can be spent on finishing touches. For example, try the elegant fruited centerpiece we demonstrate in this section.

COCKTAIL BUFFET
Roast Beef Rolls with
Lime-Jalapeño Mayonnaise
Creamed Shrimp in Pastry Shells
Rainbow Vegetable Tray   ***Black Bean Salsa***
Fruit with White Chocolate Dip
Fudge Bites

MAKE-AHEAD PLAN

To host the party with ease, follow this preparation guide.

The Day Before: Make Lime-Jalapeño Mayonnaise and Black Bean Salsa. Prepare Creamed Shrimp and refrigerate; bake pastry shells. Marinate vegetables for Rainbow Vegetable Tray, and wash lettuce leaves. Bake Fudge Bites and pipe with Kahlúa Whipped Cream; refrigerate. Wash and cut up fruit; refrigerate.

Starting 3 Hours Before the Party: Assemble fruit arrangement. Make White Chocolate Dip; let stand at room temperature. Drain vegetables; refrigerate. Remove Creamed Shrimp from refrigerator and let stand at room temperature 30 minutes. Bake Creamed Shrimp, and assemble food on serving trays, making sure garnishes are in place 30 minutes before guests arrive. Just before guests arrive, fill pastry shells with shrimp mixture.

ROAST BEEF ROLLS WITH LIME-JALAPENO MAYONNAISE

1 cup mayonnaise
½ teaspoon grated lime rind
2 teaspoons fresh lime juice
1 jalapeño pepper, seeded and chopped
3 to 3½ pounds thinly sliced roast beef
5 dozen commercial rolls

Combine first 4 ingredients; cover and refrigerate 8 hours. Serve with beef and commercial rolls. Yield: 25 appetizer servings.

Tip: A garnish gives each serving tray a final flourish. Use bunches of fresh herbs, ruffly lettuce leaves, or sliced citrus to add color and texture to each dish.

CREAMED SHRIMP IN PASTRY SHELLS

1½ pounds unpeeled medium-size fresh
     shrimp
⅔   cup Chablis or other dry white wine
2   tablespoons chopped fresh parsley
½   teaspoon salt
½   cup chopped onion
3   tablespoons butter or margarine
3   tablespoons all-purpose flour
1   cup milk
1   cup (4 ounces) shredded Swiss cheese
2   teaspoons lemon juice
½   teaspoon pepper
2   (9½-ounce) packages frozen mini
     puff pastry shells, baked

Peel and devein shrimp. Combine wine and next 3 ingredients in a saucepan; bring to a boil. Add shrimp, and cook 3 to 5 minutes; drain, reserving ¼ cup liquid. Chop shrimp and set aside.

Melt butter in a large saucepan over low heat; add flour, stirring until smooth. Cook 1 minute, stirring constantly. Gradually add milk; cook over medium heat, stirring constantly, until mixture is thickened and bubbly. Add Swiss cheese, stirring until cheese melts. Gradually stir in shrimp, reserved liquid, lemon juice, and pepper. Spoon mixture into a lightly greased 2-quart shallow baking dish. Cover and refrigerate 8 hours.

Remove baking dish from refrigerator and let stand 30 minutes at room temperature. Bake, covered, at 350° for 30 minutes or until thoroughly heated. Spoon into pastry shells. Yield: 25 appetizer servings.

Note: Four 9-inch refrigerated piecrusts may be substituted for puff pastry shells. Cut 12 (2½-inch) circles out of each pastry, and fit into miniature (1¾-inch) muffin pans; prick with a fork. Bake at 450° for 8 to 10 minutes.

RAINBOW VEGETABLE TRAY

2   (7-ounce) jars baby corn on the cob
1   (14-ounce) can artichoke hearts,
     drained and halved
1   (12-ounce) jar whole baby carrots,
     drained
2   (4.5-ounce) jars whole mushrooms,
     drained
1⅓ cups cider vinegar
⅔   cup vegetable oil
½   cup sugar
½   teaspoon salt
½   teaspoon pepper
1½ cups diced green pepper
1   cup diced purple onion
1   (4-ounce) jar diced pimiento,
     drained
     Lettuce leaves

Place each of the first 4 ingredients separately into zip-top plastic bags; set aside.

Combine vinegar and next 7 ingredients, stirring until sugar dissolves. Pour marinade equally over vegetables in plastic bags; seal securely and refrigerate 8 hours.

Drain vegetables; arrange on a lettuce-lined serving plate. Serve with wooden picks. Yield: 25 appetizer servings.

BLACK BEAN SALSA

1   (16-ounce) can black beans, rinsed
     and drained
2   tomatoes, chopped
4   green onions, sliced
1   clove garlic, crushed
3   tablespoons fresh chopped cilantro
     or 3 teaspoons dried cilantro
2½ tablespoons vegetable oil
2   tablespoons fresh lime juice
½   teaspoon ground cumin
¼   teaspoon salt
¼   teaspoon pepper

Combine all ingredients; cover and refrigerate 8 hours. Drain liquids. Serve with tortilla chips. Yield: 3 cups.

Above: Allow the party to spill over into the family room. Warm decorations and soft lighting make the room conducive to light, easy conversation.

FUDGE BITES

  2 (1-ounce) squares unsweetened
       chocolate
  ½ cup butter or margarine
  ¼ cup all-purpose flour
  1 cup sugar
  2 large eggs, beaten
       Kahlúa Whipped Cream

Combine chocolate and butter in a small heavy saucepan; cook over medium heat, stirring occasionally, until chocolate melts. Remove from heat, and stir in flour, sugar, and eggs. Spoon mixture into a greased 9-inch square pan. Bake at 350° for 18 to 20 minutes. Cool and chill. Cut into small squares; pipe or dollop with Kahlúa Whipped Cream. Store in refrigerator up to 8 hours or freeze up to 1 month. Yield: 5 dozen.

Kahlúa Whipped Cream:

  ½ cup whipping cream
  1 tablespoon sifted powdered sugar
  1 tablespoon Kahlúa

Combine all ingredients; beat at medium speed with an electric mixer until soft peaks form. Yield: 1 cup.

WHITE CHOCOLATE DIP

  2 tablespoons cornstarch
  ½ cup sugar
  ½ cup water
  1 tablespoon butter or margarine
  3 ounces white chocolate-flavored
       baking bar, coarsely chopped

Combine cornstarch, sugar, and water in a small saucepan; cook over medium heat, stirring constantly, until thickened. Remove from heat; add butter and white chocolate, stirring until chocolate melts. Let cool. Serve with fresh fruit. Yield: 1 cup.

111

Above: Some of the tools you'll need include a basket tray, craft foam, florist's foam, florist's tape, florist's water-pick tubes, 6" wooden florist's picks, and fern pins.

Above: Tape stand to basket tray and stack craft foam blocks around it. Tape florist's foam to top of stand and secure cantaloupe shell, cherub, and galax leaves.

Above: Position cantaloupe and pineapple shells around base; fill in with kale leaves. Use crumpled plastic wrap to tilt shells to desired angles.

Above: Fill fruit shells with melon balls, pineapple chunks, and White Chocolate Dip. Fill in among kale leaves with strawberries and grapes.

112

COCKTAIL BUFFET CENTERPIECE

To make this centerpiece, you'll need a stand. We used a welded-metal florist's stand, but you can also make a stand, using an 18"-long (½"-diameter) dowel and two plywood squares, 4" x 4" and 6" x 6". Drill a hole in the center of each plywood square and hot-glue the dowel in the hole.

Materials:
3 cantaloupes
melon baller
1 pineapple
stand
22"-diameter basket tray
florist's tape
3 blocks of craft foam
fern pins
1 small block of wet florist's foam
6"-diameter plastic liner
2 terra-cotta cherubs
6" wooden florist's picks
20 galax leaves
2 bunches kale
White Chocolate Dip
4 pounds of grapes
2 quarts of fresh strawberries
1 dozen roses
1 bunch safflowers
florist's water-pick tubes
bow

The day before the party, cut cantaloupes in half; discard seeds. Using a melon baller, scoop out balls. Lay pineapple on its side and cut an oval shape down to, but not through, the other side; leave stem intact. Remove cutout section and cut into cubes, discarding skin. Fill center of fruit shells with paper towels; place in heavy-duty, zip-top plastic bags and refrigerate. Place melon balls and cubed pineapple in airtight containers or plastic bags and refrigerate.

To make the arrangement, position stand on basket tray and secure with florist's tape. Arrange craft foam on stand and secure with fern pins. Place wet florist's foam in plastic liner and secure to top of stand with florist's tape. Place cherub on

Above: Place flowers in water picks and insert into craft foam around stand and at sides of arrangement. Gold foil bow can simply rest on kale and galax leaves.

florist's foam and secure by wrapping tape around cherub's neck and taping to plastic liner.

Secure 1 cantaloupe shell to florist's foam with several wooden picks, leaving ½" of each pick showing, to keep cantaloupe from slipping. Attach galax leaves to foam with fern pins to cover remaining foam.

At base of stand, secure 1 cantaloupe shell to top block of craft foam, using wooden picks. Position 2 cantaloupe shells and pineapple shell on basket, using folded plastic wrap to give desired tilt. Stuff kale leaves around shells.

Fill fruit shells with melon balls, pineapple chunks, and White Chocolate Dip. Fill in around shells with grapes and strawberries. Place flowers in water-pick tubes filled with water and insert into arrangement, pushing 4 roses down into center around stand. Arrange additional flowers as desired. Add bow and second cherub.

113

Breads

WHEAT-SOUR CREAM ROLLS

½ cup butter or margarine
1 (8-ounce) carton sour cream
½ cup firmly packed brown sugar
1 teaspoon salt
2 packages dry yeast
½ cup warm water (105° to 115°)
2 large eggs, beaten
2½ cups all-purpose flour
1⅓ cups whole wheat flour
3 tablespoons wheat germ
¼ teaspoon ground cardamom
¼ cup butter or margarine, melted

Combine first 4 ingredients in a small saucepan; cook over low heat until butter melts, stirring occasionally. Cool to 105° to 115°.

Dissolve yeast in warm water in a large bowl; let stand 5 minutes. Stir in sour cream mixture and beaten eggs.

Combine flours, wheat germ, and cardamom; gradually add to yeast mixture, stirring well. Cover and refrigerate at least 8 hours.

Punch dough down, and shape into desired rolls:

Crescents: Divide dough into 4 portions. Roll each portion into a 10-inch circle on a floured surface, and brush with 1 tablespoon melted butter. Cut each circle into 12 wedges; roll each wedge, jellyroll fashion, beginning at wide end. Place on greased baking sheets, point side down. Cover and let rise in a warm place (85°), free from drafts, 45 minutes or until doubled in bulk. Bake at 375° for 10 minutes or until golden brown. Yield: 4 dozen.

Pan Rolls: Lightly grease two 9-inch round cakepans. Shape dough into 1½-inch balls. Place

16 dough balls in each pan, leaving about ½-inch space between them. Cover and let rise in a warm place (85°), free from drafts, until doubled in bulk. Bake at 375° for 15 to 20 minutes. Brush with ¼ cup melted butter. Yield: 32 rolls.

Cloverleaf Rolls: Lightly grease muffin pans. Shape dough into 1-inch balls; place 3 dough balls in each muffin cup. Cover and let rise in a warm place (85°), free from drafts, until doubled in bulk. Bake at 375° for 10 to 12 minutes. Brush with ¼ cup melted butter. Yield: 32 rolls.

Crescents: Roll wedges from wide end toward point.

Pan rolls: Place 1½-inch balls of dough ½ inch apart in pan.

Cloverleaf rolls: Place three 1-inch balls of dough in each muffin cup.

Opposite: Fond memories of hearth and home linger in the scent of bread baking. Wheat-Sour Cream Rolls are especially delicious when enjoyed with Basil Jelly (recipe on page 134).

GINGER-CHEESE MUFFINS

2 cups all-purpose flour
1 tablespoon baking powder
¼ teaspoon baking soda
¼ teaspoon salt
¼ teaspoon ground ginger
1 large egg, beaten
½ cup milk
½ cup molasses
¼ cup vegetable oil
¾ cup (3 ounces) shredded mild cheese
  Vegetable cooking spray

Combine first 5 ingredients in a large bowl; make a well in center of mixture. Combine egg and next 3 ingredients; add to dry ingredients, stirring just until moistened. Fold in cheese.

Place paper liners in muffin pans, and coat with cooking spray; spoon batter into liners, filling two-thirds full. Bake at 425° for 10 minutes. Remove from pans immediately. Yield: 16 muffins.

TEA BISCUITS

2 cups butter, softened
1 cup sugar
5 large eggs
1 tablespoon vanilla extract
5½ cups unbleached flour
2 tablespoons baking powder
½ teaspoon salt
1 large egg, lightly beaten
  Sesame seeds (optional)

Beat butter at medium speed with an electric mixer until fluffy; gradually add sugar, beating well. Add 5 eggs, one at a time, beating after each addition. Stir in vanilla.

Combine flour, baking powder, and salt; add to creamed mixture, mixing well. Cover and chill 2 hours.

Shape dough into walnut-size pieces; roll each piece into a 4-inch rope. Fold each rope in half and twist; place on lightly greased baking sheets. Brush with beaten egg; sprinkle with sesame

seeds, if desired. Bake at 350° for 20 minutes or until lightly browned. Cool slightly; transfer to wire racks to cool completely. Store in an airtight container. Yield: 8 dozen.

CHERRY-BUTTERSCOTCH RING

½ cup firmly packed brown sugar
¼ cup butter or margarine, melted
1 tablespoon light corn syrup
½ cup chopped walnuts
½ cup red candied cherries, halved
1 package dry yeast
¾ cup warm water (105° to 115°)
2¼ cups all-purpose flour, divided
¼ cup sugar
¼ cup shortening
1 large egg, beaten
1 teaspoon salt

Combine first 3 ingredients; spoon into a greased 6-cup ring mold. Sprinkle with walnuts and cherries; set aside.

Dissolve yeast in warm water in a large bowl; let stand 5 minutes. Add 1 cup flour and next 4 ingredients; beat at medium speed with an electric mixer 2 minutes or until smooth. Gradually stir in remaining flour. Drop by small spoonfuls onto walnuts and cherries. Cover and let rise in a warm place (85°), free from drafts, about 1 hour or until doubled in bulk. Bake at 375° for 25 minutes or until browned. Immediately invert onto serving platter. Yield: one 9-inch coffee cake.

COFFEE CAKE INTERNATIONAL

¾ cup butter or margarine, softened
1½ cups sugar
3 large eggs
½ teaspoon almond extract
3 cups all-purpose flour
1½ teaspoons baking soda
1 (8-ounce) carton sour cream
  Vegetable cooking spray
1 (21-ounce) can cherry pie filling
  Streusel Topping

Beat butter at medium speed with an electric mixer until fluffy; gradually add sugar, beating well. Add eggs, one at a time, beating after each addition. Stir in almond extract.

Combine flour and soda; add to creamed mixture alternately with sour cream, beginning and ending with flour mixture. Mix after each addition.

Pour batter into two 9-inch round cakepans coated with cooking spray. Spoon half of cherry pie filling on top of batter to within ¼ inch from edge of each pan. Sprinkle with Streusel Topping. Bake at 350° for 35 to 40 minutes or until a wooden pick inserted in center comes out clean. Yield: two 9-inch coffee cakes.

Streusel Topping:

½ cup all-purpose flour
¼ cup sugar
½ teaspoon ground cinnamon
¼ cup butter

Combine first 3 ingredients; cut in butter with pastry blender until mixture is crumbly. Yield: about 1 cup.

ORANGE-RAISIN BREAD

2 packages dry yeast
1½ cups warm water (105° to 115°)
4¼ to 4¾ cups all-purpose flour, divided
½ cup sugar
1 teaspoon salt
¼ cup butter or margarine, softened
1 large egg
1 egg white
2 tablespoons grated orange rind
½ cup raisins
1 egg yolk
2 tablespoons water
¼ cup firmly packed brown sugar
3 tablespoons coarsely chopped pecans
2 teaspoons grated orange rind

Dissolve yeast in warm water in a large bowl; let stand 5 minutes. Add 3 cups flour and next 6 ingredients. Beat at low speed with an electric

mixer until blended. Beat an additional 2 minutes at medium speed. Gradually stir in enough remaining flour to make a medium-stiff dough. Stir in raisins. Cover and let rise in a warm place (85°), free from drafts, 1 hour or until doubled in bulk.

Punch dough down; spoon evenly into a lightly greased and floured 2½-quart soufflé dish. Combine egg yolk and water; brush over dough. Combine brown sugar, pecans, and 2 teaspoons orange rind; sprinkle evenly over dough, pressing in gently. Bake at 375° for 50 to 55 minutes or until loaf sounds hollow when tapped, shielding with aluminum foil after 20 minutes. Remove from dish immediately, and cool on a wire rack. Yield: 1 loaf.

CRANBERRY SURPRISE LOAF

2 (3-ounce) packages cream cheese, softened
1 large egg
¼ cup sugar
¼ teaspoon vanilla extract
2 cups all-purpose flour
2 teaspoons baking powder
½ teaspoon salt
1 cup sugar
1 large egg, lightly beaten
¾ cup apple juice
¼ cup butter or margarine, melted
1½ cups chopped fresh cranberries
½ cup chopped pecans

Combine first 4 ingredients in a small bowl; beat at medium speed with an electric mixer until smooth. Set aside. Combine flour and next 3 ingredients in a large bowl; make a well in center of mixture. Combine 1 egg, apple juice, and butter; add to dry ingredients, stirring just until moistened. Fold in cranberries and pecans.

Spoon half of batter into a greased and floured 9- x 5- x 3-inch loafpan. Spread cream cheese mixture over batter, and top with remaining batter. Bake at 375° for 1 hour and 5 minutes or until a wooden pick inserted in center comes out clean, shielding with aluminum foil after 45 minutes. Cool in pan 10 minutes; remove from pan and cool on a wire rack. Yield: 1 loaf.

GOLDEN HOLIDAY BREAD

¾ **cup milk**
½ **cup butter or margarine**
¼ **cup water**
3 **cups all-purpose flour,**
  divided
½ **cup sugar**
1 **package dry yeast**
½ **teaspoon salt**
3 **egg yolks**
1 **cup golden raisins**
¼ **cup sugar**
¼ **cup water**
2 **tablespoons lemon juice**

Combine milk, butter, and ¼ cup water in a small saucepan; cook over low heat until butter melts, stirring occasionally. Cool to 120° to 130°.

Combine 1½ cups flour, ½ cup sugar, yeast, and salt in a large mixing bowl. Gradually add liquid mixture to flour mixture, beating at low speed with an electric mixer. Beat an additional 2 minutes at medium speed. Add ½ cup flour and egg yolks; beat 2 minutes at high speed. Gradually stir in remaining flour and raisins (dough will be sticky). Cover and let rise in a warm place (85°), free from drafts, 1 hour (dough will not double in bulk).

Punch dough down; spoon into a greased 12-cup Bundt pan. Cover and let rise in a warm place, free from drafts, about 1 hour. Bake at 350° for 35 minutes or until golden brown. Remove bread from pan immediately.

Combine ¼ cup sugar, ¼ cup water, and lemon juice, stirring until sugar dissolves. Brush glaze over warm bread; let cool completely on a wire rack. Yield: 1 loaf.

Above: Slightly sweet Golden Holiday Bread is the perfect light breakfast to enjoy Christmas morning before beginning all the excitement of the day.

Confections

PEPPERMINT-CHOCOLATE TRUFFLES

¾ cup butter
1 ½ cups sugar
  1 (5-ounce) can evaporated milk
  1 (10-ounce) package mint-flavored chocolate morsels
  1 (7-ounce) jar marshmallow cream
  1 teaspoon vanilla extract
  6 (2-ounce) squares vanilla-flavored candy coating
⅓ cup semisweet chocolate morsels
  2 (2-ounce) squares vanilla-flavored candy coating, melted (optional)
   Green paste food coloring (optional)

Combine butter, sugar, and evaporated milk in a large saucepan; bring to a boil, stirring constantly. Reduce heat and simmer, stirring constantly, until mixture reaches 234°. Remove from heat; add mint-flavored chocolate morsels, stirring until chocolate melts. Stir in marshmallow cream and vanilla.

Spoon mixture into a lightly greased 15- x 10- x 1-inch jellyroll pan; chill 1 hour. Cut into 96 squares, and roll each square into a ball; chill.

Combine 6 squares vanilla-flavored candy coating and semisweet chocolate morsels in a heavy saucepan. Cook over low heat until coating melts, stirring occasionally. Remove from heat and cool slightly. Dip half of truffles in mixture, keeping remaining half in refrigerator; place on wax paper to cool. Repeat with remaining half of truffles.

Combine two 2-ounce squares of melted candy coating and food coloring, and drizzle over truffles, if desired. Store in refrigerator. Yield: 8 dozen.

Note: Do not substitute green liquid food coloring for green paste food coloring. Paste food coloring can be found in specialty craft stores or ordered by mail (see Resources, page 156).

Above: This luscious assortment of confections will satisfy any sweet-tooth craving. Shown here are Peppermint-Chocolate Truffles, Peanut Butter Squares, and Raspberry Divinity.

PEANUT BUTTER SQUARES

1 cup butter or margarine
1 cup chunky peanut butter
2 cups graham cracker crumbs
2 cups sifted powdered sugar
1 cup semisweet chocolate morsels
2 tablespoons shortening

Combine butter and peanut butter in a 2-quart glass bowl. Cover with a paper towel, and microwave at HIGH 1½ minutes. Stir in graham cracker crumbs and powdered sugar. Press mixture into an 11- x 7½- x 1½-inch dish.

Combine chocolate morsels and shortening in a 2-cup glass measure; microwave at MEDIUM (50% power) 2 minutes or until chocolate melts. Spread over peanut butter mixture. Chill and cut into squares. Yield: 4 dozen.

RASPBERRY DIVINITY

3 cups sugar
¾ cup water
¾ cup light corn syrup
¼ teaspoon salt
2 egg whites
1 (3-ounce) package raspberry-flavored
   gelatin
1 cup chopped slivered almonds,
   toasted

Combine first 4 ingredients in a heavy 3-quart saucepan; cook over low heat, stirring gently, until sugar dissolves. Cover and cook over medium heat 2 to 3 minutes to wash down sugar crystals from sides of pan. Uncover and cook over medium heat, without stirring, to hard ball stage (258°). Remove from heat.

Beat egg whites in a large bowl at high speed with an electric mixer until foamy. Add gelatin, and beat until stiff peaks form. Gradually pour hot syrup mixture in a thin stream over egg whites while beating constantly at high speed until mixture holds its shape (3 to 4 minutes). Quickly stir in almonds, and drop mixture by rounded teaspoonfuls onto wax paper. Let cool. Yield: 3 dozen.

SHORTCUT PECAN PRALINES

1 (3-ounce) package vanilla
   pudding mix
1½ cups firmly packed brown sugar
1 (5-ounce) can evaporated milk
1 tablespoon butter or margarine
1 teaspoon vanilla extract
2 cups pecan halves

Combine first 5 ingredients in a large saucepan. Cook over low heat, stirring gently, until sugar dissolves. Cook over medium heat, without stirring, to 232°. Remove from heat; add pecans, and beat with a wooden spoon just until mixture begins to thicken (about 2 minutes). Working rapidly, drop by tablespoonfuls onto lightly greased wax paper; let stand until firm. Yield: 2 dozen.

CHOCOLAVA

1 (17¼-ounce) package frozen phyllo
   pastry, thawed
1 cup butter or margarine, melted
1 pound finely chopped walnuts
1 cup semisweet chocolate mini-morsels
¾ cup sugar
1½ teaspoons ground cinnamon
¾ cup orange juice
½ cup sugar
½ cup water
½ cup honey
1 tablespoon lemon juice
1 (1-ounce) square semisweet chocolate
1½ teaspoons water

Cut phyllo to fit a 15- x 10- x 1-inch jellyroll pan. Cover phyllo with a slightly damp towel.

Lightly butter bottom of a 15- x 10- x 1-inch pan. Layer 8 sheets of phyllo in pan, brushing each sheet with melted butter. Set aside.

Combine walnuts, chocolate morsels, ¾ cup sugar, and cinnamon, mixing well. Sprinkle one-third of nut mixture over phyllo in pan. Top with 4 sheets of phyllo, brushing each sheet with melted butter. Sprinkle with another third of nut mixture. Repeat procedure with phyllo and remaining nut mixture. Top with remaining sheets of phyllo, brushing each sheet with melted butter. Cut into diamond-shape pieces. Brush with remaining butter. Bake at 325° for 45 minutes or until golden.

While Chocolava is baking, combine orange juice and next 4 ingredients in a saucepan. Bring mixture to a boil; reduce heat, and simmer 20 minutes. Pour over warm Chocolava. Cool completely.

Combine 1-ounce square semisweet chocolate and 1½ teaspoons water in a small microwave-safe bowl. Microwave on MEDIUM (50% power) 1 to 2 minutes or until chocolate melts, stirring after 1 minute. Drizzle over Chocolava. Yield: about 6½ dozen.

Note: Butter-flavored vegetable cooking spray may be substituted for melted butter between layers of phyllo.

APRICOT-CHOCOLATE CHIP COOKIES

¼ cup butter or margarine, softened
¼ cup shortening
⅓ cup sugar
⅓ cup firmly packed brown sugar
1 large egg
½ teaspoon vanilla extract
1 cup all-purpose flour
½ teaspoon baking soda
½ teaspoon salt
⅔ cup finely chopped dried apricots
½ cup semisweet chocolate morsels
¼ cup chopped pecans

Beat butter and shortening in a large bowl at medium speed with an electric mixer; gradually add sugars, beating well. Add egg and vanilla, mixing well.

Combine flour, soda, and salt; gradually add to creamed mixture, mixing well. Stir in apricots and remaining ingredients.

Drop dough by rounded teaspoonfuls onto lightly greased cookie sheets. Bake at 350° for 10 minutes or until lightly browned. Cool on wire racks. Yield: 4 dozen.

APPLE PIE BARS

2 cups all-purpose flour
½ teaspoon baking powder
½ teaspoon salt
½ cup sugar
1 cup butter or margarine
2 egg yolks, lightly beaten
2 cups peeled and thinly sliced cooking apples
½ cup sugar
¼ cup all-purpose flour
1 teaspoon ground cinnamon
¼ teaspoon ground nutmeg
2 egg whites, lightly beaten
Glaze

Combine first 4 ingredients. Cut butter into flour mixture with a pastry blender until mixture is crumbly. Stir in egg yolks (mixture will be crumbly). Press half of mixture into bottom of a lightly greased 13- x 9- x 2-inch pan.

Combine apples and next 4 ingredients; arrange over crust. Crumble reserved crust mixture over apples; press gently. Brush with egg whites. Bake at 350° for 40 minutes. Let cool in pan. Drizzle with Glaze. Yield: 4 dozen.

Glaze:

1 cup sifted powdered sugar
2 tablespoons milk
1 teaspoon vanilla extract

Combine all ingredients, stirring well. Yield: about ⅓ cup.

TINY CHRISTMAS BITES

⅓ cup butter or margarine, melted
1 cup graham cracker crumbs
1 (14-ounce) can sweetened condensed milk
2 cups chopped pecans
1 cup chopped dates
1 (6-ounce) package frozen coconut, thawed
½ cup candied cherries, chopped
½ cup candied pineapple, chopped
1 teaspoon vanilla extract
1 teaspoon almond extract

Combine butter and graham cracker crumbs; add sweetened condensed milk and remaining ingredients, stirring until blended. Spoon 1 tablespoon into each cup of paper-lined miniature (1¾-inch) muffin pans. Bake at 325° for 25 to 30 minutes. Remove from pans, and cool completely on wire racks. Yield: 6 dozen.

Tip: If cookies won't slip off the cookie sheet without crumbling, try warming the cookie sheet in the oven for 1 to 2 minutes.

Tasty sweets for the season include, clockwise from top, Shortbread Cookies, Christmas Tree Sandwich Cookies, and Tiny Christmas Bites.

CHRISTMAS TREE SANDWICH COOKIES

1¼ cups butter or margarine, softened
⅔ cup sugar
2 cups all-purpose flour
1 cup ground almonds
¾ cup ground hazelnuts, toasted
1 teaspoon ground cinnamon
⅔ cup seedless raspberry jam

Beat butter at medium speed with an electric mixer until fluffy; gradually add sugar, beating well. Gradually add flour, ground nuts, and cinnamon; beat at low speed just until dry ingredients are moistened. (Dough will be crumbly.) Divide dough in half, and shape into a ball. Wrap each portion, and chill at least 1 hour.

Roll one portion to ⅛-inch thickness on a lightly floured surface. Cut with a 3-inch tree-shaped cutter, and place on lightly greased cookie sheets. Bake at 350° for 7 to 9 minutes or until lightly browned. Cool on wire racks.

Repeat procedure with remaining dough. Before baking, cut small holes in cookies using a drinking straw. Bake as above, and cool on wire racks. Spread top of solid cookie with 1 teaspoon jam; top each with cutout cookie. Yield: 2½ dozen.

SHORTBREAD COOKIES

¾ cup butter, softened
½ cup sugar
1 egg yolk
1½ cups all-purpose flour
½ teaspoon vanilla extract
Pecan halves

Beat butter at medium speed with an electric mixer until fluffy; gradually add sugar, beating well. Add egg yolk, beating well. Add flour, mixing well. Stir in vanilla. Shape dough into 1-inch balls, and place on ungreased cookie sheets. Gently press a pecan half in center of each cookie. Bake at 300° for 14 to 16 minutes or until lightly browned. Cool 5 minutes; transfer to wire racks to cool completely. Yield: 6 dozen.

123

Beverages

APRICOT SLUSH

2 (46-ounce) cans apricot nectar
1 (46-ounce) can pineapple juice
2 (12-ounce) cans frozen orange juice concentrate, thawed and undiluted
1 (6-ounce) can frozen lemonade concentrate, thawed and undiluted
1 (67.6-ounce) bottle ginger ale, chilled

Combine first 4 ingredients in a large plastic container; freeze until firm.

Remove punch from freezer 1½ hours before serving. Place mixture in a punch bowl, and break into chunks. Add ginger ale; stir until slushy. Yield: about 7 quarts.

CRANBERRY FRUIT PUNCH

1 (48-ounce) bottle cranberry juice cocktail, chilled
1 (46-ounce) can unsweetened pink grapefruit juice, chilled
1 (33.8-ounce) bottle ginger ale, chilled

Combine all ingredients; serve over ice. Yield: 1 gallon.

ORANGE PUNCH

2 (0.15-ounce) packages unsweetened orange-flavored drink mix
1 cup sugar
2 quarts water
1 (46-ounce) can unsweetened pineapple juice
½ gallon orange sherbet, softened
1 (67.6-ounce) bottle ginger ale, chilled

Combine first 4 ingredients; chill. Just before serving, spoon sherbet into punch bowl. Slowly pour chilled mixture and ginger ale over sherbet, stirring gently. Serve immediately. Yield: 7½ quarts.

SANTA'S QUENCHER

2 (6-ounce) cans frozen limeade concentrate, thawed and undiluted
1 (12-ounce) can frozen lemonade concentrate, thawed and undiluted
1 cup sifted powdered sugar
7 cups crushed ice
4 drops of green food coloring (optional)
4 (10-ounce) bottles club soda

Combine half each of first 4 ingredients in container of an electric blender; add 2 drops of food coloring, if desired. Blend at high speed until slushy. Pour into a large heavy-duty zip-top plastic bag; freeze. Repeat procedure with remaining half of ingredients and food coloring, if desired. Remove each bag from freezer 30 minutes before serving. Place in serving container, and break into chunks; add 2 bottles club soda to each bag of mixture. Stir until slushy. Yield: about 3 quarts or 1½ quarts per bag of mixture.

HOT BUTTERED COFFEE

½ cup butter or margarine, softened
⅓ cup sifted powdered sugar
¾ teaspoon ground cinnamon
1 pint vanilla ice cream, softened
3 cups strong brewed coffee

Combine first 3 ingredients in a mixing bowl; beat at medium speed with an electric mixer until smooth. Add ice cream, beating well. Spoon mixture into a freezer-proof container, and freeze.

To serve, place ⅓ cup butter mixture in a cup. Add ½ cup hot coffee; stir well. Serve immediately. Yield: 6 cups.

BRANDY COCOA

3 tablespoons sugar
3 tablespoons cocoa
Dash of salt
4 cups milk
¼ cup brandy

Combine first 3 ingredients in a medium saucepan; add milk, stirring until blended. Cook over medium heat until hot (do not boil); stir in brandy. Serve hot. Yield: 4¼ cups.

ICY BOURBON TEA

2 cups boiling water
5 regular-size tea bags
1½ cups sugar
1 (6-ounce) can frozen lemonade concentrate, thawed and undiluted
1 (6-ounce) can frozen orange juice concentrate, thawed and undiluted
5 cups water
2 cups bourbon
1 (33.8-ounce) bottle ginger ale, chilled

Pour 2 cups boiling water over tea bags; cover and steep 5 minutes. Remove tea bags, squeezing gently; stir in sugar and next 4 ingredients. Cover and freeze until firm.

Remove punch from freezer 1 hour before serving. Place mixture in punch bowl, and break into chunks. Add ginger ale; stir until slushy. Yield: 4½ quarts.

Above: What beverage could be more synonymous with Christmas than eggnog? Mocha Eggnog is sure to become a family favorite.

SPIRITED COFFEE PUNCH

2 quarts boiling water
⅓ cup instant coffee granules
¼ cup sugar
1 cup Kahlúa or other coffee-flavored liqueur
2 cups milk
1 teaspoon vanilla extract
1 quart vanilla ice cream, softened
Whipped cream (optional)

Combine first 3 ingredients, stirring until coffee dissolves; chill. Add Kahlúa and next 3 ingredients, stirring until blended. Ladle beverage into cups. Top with whipped cream, if desired. Yield: 3½ quarts.

MOCHA EGGNOG

1 teaspoon instant coffee granules
½ cup hot water
1 (32-ounce) carton commercial refrigerated eggnog
¼ to ½ cup brandy
½ cup chocolate syrup
½ cup whipping cream, whipped
Grated semisweet chocolate (optional)

Dissolve coffee granules in water; let cool.

Combine coffee, eggnog, brandy, and chocolate syrup. Cover and refrigerate. To serve, fold in whipped cream, and garnish with grated chocolate, if desired. Yield: about 6 cups.

125

Frosty, sophisticated Raspberry-Beaujolais Sorbet makes the perfect light ending for a rich meal.

Desserts

RASPBERRY-BEAUJOLAIS SORBET

  3 cups frozen raspberries, thawed
½ cup water
¾ cup sugar
  1 cup Beaujolais or other dry red wine
¼ cup whipping cream
  2 tablespoons lemon juice

Combine raspberries and water in container of an electric blender or food processor; process until smooth. Pour mixture through a wire-mesh strainer, pressing raspberries with back of spoon against the sides of the strainer to squeeze out juice. Discard pulp and seeds remaining in strainer. Return to blender; add sugar and remaining ingredients, and process 1 minute. Pour mixture into a 9-inch square pan; freeze until almost firm.

Break mixture into chunks, and place in a large mixing bowl; beat at low speed with an electric mixer until smooth. Return to pan, and freeze until firm. Yield: 3 cups.

LEMON MOUSSE

  1 (8-ounce) carton egg substitute
½ cup sugar
    Dash of salt
  1 tablespoon grated lemon rind
½ cup lemon juice
  1 (1.3-ounce) envelope whipped topping mix
    Frozen whipped topping, thawed (optional)

Combine first 5 ingredients in a heavy saucepan. Cook over medium heat, stirring constantly, about 6 minutes or until mixture begins to thicken. Chill.

Prepare whipped topping mix according to package directions; fold into custard mixture. Spoon into parfait glasses, and chill 3 hours. Top with a dollop of whipped topping, if desired. Yield: 6 servings.

COCONUT CREAM CHEESECAKE

1⅔ cups graham cracker crumbs
¼ cup sugar
¼ cup plus 2 tablespoons butter or margarine, melted
3 (8-ounce) packages cream cheese, softened
1½ cups sugar
4 large eggs
2 egg yolks
1 cup flaked coconut
1 cup whipping cream
1 teaspoon vanilla extract
¼ to ½ teaspoon coconut flavoring
Whipped cream (optional)
Toasted coconut (optional)

Combine first 3 ingredients; firmly press evenly onto bottom and 2 inches up sides of a 10-inch springform pan.

Beat cream cheese at high speed with an electric mixer until light and fluffy; gradually add 1½ cups sugar, beating well. Add eggs and yolks, one at a time, beating after each addition. Stir in coconut and next 3 ingredients; pour into prepared crust. Bake at 325° for 1 hour and 10 minutes. (Center will be soft.) Turn oven off, and leave cake in oven 30 minutes. Remove from oven, and let cool to room temperature on a wire rack. Cover and chill at least 8 hours.

Carefully remove sides of pan. If desired, top each serving with whipped cream, and sprinkle with toasted coconut. Yield: 10 to 12 servings.

STRAWBERRY-GLAZED CHRISTMAS CAKE

(pictured on page 99)
1 cup butter or margarine, softened
1 cup sugar
6 large eggs, separated
2 cups sifted cake flour
½ teaspoon baking powder
½ teaspoon salt
¾ cup sugar
3 cups whipping cream
2 tablespoons powdered sugar
1 teaspoon vanilla extract
1 (12-ounce) jar strawberry preserves (about 1 cup), divided
1½ cups chopped pecans

Beat butter at medium speed with an electric mixer until fluffy; gradually add 1 cup sugar, beating well. Add egg yolks, one at a time, beating after each addition.

Combine flour, baking powder, and salt; gradually add to creamed mixture. Mix just until blended.

Beat egg whites until foamy. Gradually add ¾ cup sugar, beating until stiff peaks form; fold into batter. Spoon batter into three greased and floured 9-inch round cakepans. Bake at 350° for 18 to 20 minutes or until a wooden pick inserted in center comes out clean. Cool in pans on wire racks 10 minutes; remove from pans, and let cool completely on wire racks.

Beat whipping cream until foamy; gradually add powdered sugar and vanilla, beating until soft peaks form.

Stack layers, spreading 1 cup whipped cream between each layer, and drizzling ⅓ cup strawberry preserves on whipped cream between each layer. Spread top and sides with remaining whipped cream. Carefully pat pecans around sides.

Place remaining strawberry preserves in container of an electric blender, and process until smooth. Pour pureed preserves into zip-top plastic bag with a small hole cut in bottom corner. Drizzle lines of preserves on top of cake about 1½ inches apart. Carefully pull a wooden pick through lines at 1-inch intervals.

Store in refrigerator. Yield: one 3-layer cake.

APPLE LANE CAKE

 1 cup butter or margarine, softened
 2 cups sugar
3¼ cups all-purpose flour
 1 tablespoon baking powder
 ¾ teaspoon salt
 ½ teaspoon ground cinnamon
 1 cup milk
 1 teaspoon vanilla extract
 ½ cup peeled, shredded red apple
 8 egg whites, stiffly beaten
   Apple Filling
   Boiled Frosting

Beat butter at medium speed with an electric mixer until fluffy; gradually add sugar, beating well. Combine flour and next 3 ingredients; add to creamed mixture alternately with milk, beginning and ending with flour mixture. Mix after each addition. Stir in vanilla and shredded apple. Fold in egg whites.

Pour batter into three greased and floured 9-inch round cakepans. Bake at 350° for 20 minutes or until a wooden pick inserted in center comes out clean. Cool in pans on wire racks 10 minutes; remove from pans, and let cool completely on wire racks. Spread Apple Filling between cake layers and on top of cake, leaving a 1-inch border around edge; spread Boiled Frosting around edge and on sides of cake. Yield: one 3-layer cake.

Apple Filling:

 8 egg yolks
 1 cup sugar
 ¼ teaspoon salt
 ½ cup bourbon
 ⅓ cup butter or margarine, melted
 1 teaspoon vanilla extract
 1 cup chopped pecans
 2 cups peeled, chopped red apple

Combine first 3 ingredients in top of a double boiler; beat at high speed with an electric mixer until thick and pale. Gradually add bourbon and butter, beating until blended.

Place over boiling water; cook, stirring constantly, until mixture thickens and reaches 160° (about 15 to 20 minutes). Remove from heat; stir in vanilla and pecans. Cover and chill. Stir in 2 cups chopped apple. Yield: 4 cups.

Boiled Frosting:

 ⅓ cup sugar
 ¼ cup light corn syrup
 2 tablespoons water
 2 egg whites
 1 teaspoon vanilla extract

Combine first 3 ingredients in a small heavy saucepan; cook over medium heat, stirring constantly, until clear. Cover and cook 2 minutes. Uncover and cook, without stirring, to 242°.

Beat egg whites at high speed with an electric mixer until soft peaks form; continue to beat, slowly adding hot syrup in a steady stream. Add vanilla, and continue beating until stiff peaks form and frosting is thick enough to spread. Yield: 2 cups.

SOUTHERN FRUITCAKE

 2 cups butter or margarine, softened
 2 cups sugar
 1 dozen large eggs
 ½ pound red candied cherries, chopped
 ½ pound green candied cherries, chopped
 1 pound candied pineapple, chopped
 1 pound pecans, chopped
 1 (15-ounce) package golden raisins
 2 (8-ounce) packages whole pitted dates, chopped
 1 (8-ounce) package dried figs, chopped
 4 cups all-purpose flour, divided
 1 tablespoon ground cinnamon
 1 tablespoon ground allspice
 1 (16-ounce) jar grape jam

Line three 9- x 5- x 3-inch loafpans with brown paper. (Do not use recycled paper.) Grease and set aside.

Beat butter at medium speed with an electric mixer until fluffy; gradually add sugar, beating well. Add eggs, one at a time, beating after each addition.

Combine red and green candied cherries and next 5 ingredients in a large bowl; dredge with 2 cups flour, stirring to coat well. Combine remaining 2 cups flour, cinnamon, and allspice; add to creamed mixture. Gradually add dredged fruit and jam, stirring well.

Spoon batter into prepared pans. Bake at 250° for 3½ hours. Cool in pans on wire racks. Remove cakes from pans, and remove paper liners. Store in airtight containers in a cool place. Yield: three 9-inch loaves.

CRANBERRY CAKE

3 cups all-purpose flour
1 teaspoon baking soda
¼ teaspoon salt
1 cup vegetable oil
1 cup buttermilk
2 large eggs
2 cups sugar
2 cups fresh or frozen cranberries, thawed
1 cup chopped pecans
1 cup whole, pitted dates, chopped
1 tablespoon grated orange rind
   Orange Glaze

Combine first 3 ingredients; set aside.

Combine oil and next 3 ingredients; beat at medium speed with an electric mixer until blended. Add flour mixture; beat at low speed just until blended. Stir in cranberries and next 3 ingredients. Spoon batter into a greased and floured 12-cup Bundt pan. Bake at 350° for 1 hour and 5 minutes or until a wooden pick inserted in center comes out clean. Cool in pan on a wire rack 10 minutes; remove from pan, and place on serving plate. Immediately brush with warm Orange Glaze. Yield: one 10-inch cake.

Orange Glaze:

¼ cup orange juice
¼ cup sugar

Combine orange juice and sugar in a small saucepan; bring to a boil, stirring until sugar dissolves. Yield: ⅓ cup.

APPLE PIE WITH WALNUT TOPPING

4 cups peeled, thinly sliced cooking apples (about 4 apples)
1 tablespoon lemon juice
¾ cup whipping cream
¾ cup sugar
1½ tablespoons quick-cooking tapioca
⅛ teaspoon salt
½ teaspoon ground cinnamon
¼ teaspoon ground nutmeg
   Pastry for one 9-inch pie
   Walnut Crumb Topping

Combine first 3 ingredients; let stand 15 minutes.

Combine sugar and next 4 ingredients; add to apple mixture, stirring well. Spoon into pastry shell. Bake at 425° for 10 minutes; sprinkle with Walnut Crumb Topping. Reduce temperature to 350°, and bake an additional 30 minutes. Serve with ice cream. Yield: one 9-inch pie.

Walnut Crumb Topping:

½ cup firmly packed brown sugar
½ cup graham cracker crumbs
¼ cup all-purpose flour
¼ cup chopped walnuts
½ teaspoon ground cinnamon
¼ cup butter or margarine, melted

Combine first 5 ingredients; add butter, stirring well. Yield: about 1¼ cups.

MACADAMIA PIE

3 large eggs, lightly beaten
⅔ cup sugar
1 cup dark corn syrup
1 cup finely chopped macadamia nuts
¼ cup butter or margarine, melted
1 unbaked 9-inch pastry shell
Rum Syrup

Combine first 3 ingredients; stir in macadamia nuts and butter. Pour into pastry shell. Bake at 350° for 30 to 35 minutes or until set. Cool on wire rack. Serve with Rum Syrup. Yield: one 9-inch pie.

Rum Syrup:

2 tablespoons butter or margarine
½ cup firmly packed brown sugar
¼ cup dark corn syrup
2 tablespoons light rum
1 teaspoon vanilla extract

Melt butter in a saucepan over medium heat; stir in brown sugar and corn syrup. Cook until sugar dissolves and mixture comes to a boil, stirring constantly. Remove from heat; stir in rum and vanilla. Serve warm. Yield: ⅔ cup.

CARAMEL-ICE CREAM TART

¾ cup firmly packed brown sugar
1 large egg
2 tablespoons butter or margarine, melted
1 teaspoon vanilla extract
⅛ teaspoon salt
⅓ cup all-purpose flour
¼ teaspoon baking soda
1 cup chopped pecans
½ gallon vanilla ice cream, softened
Nutty Caramel Sauce

Line a 9-inch springform pan smoothly with aluminum foil, folding edges over rim. Generously coat foil with butter.

Combine first 5 ingredients; add flour and soda, stirring until blended. Stir in pecans, and spread over bottom of prepared pan. Bake at 350° for 25 minutes or until edges are barely firm. Cool in pan. Gently loosen foil from pan, and lift shell from pan; carefully remove foil. Wrap shell in foil until ready to serve.

Line same 9-inch springform pan with foil or plastic wrap. Spread ice cream in pan, and freeze. Lift ice cream from pan; remove foil. To serve, place cookie crust on serving platter; top with ice cream layer. Cut into serving pieces, and drizzle with Nutty Caramel Sauce. Yield: one 9-inch tart.

Nutty Caramel Sauce:

1 cup sugar
½ cup butter or margarine
½ cup half-and-half
½ cup chopped pecans, toasted

Sprinkle sugar in a large cast-iron skillet. Cook over medium heat, stirring constantly with a wooden spoon until sugar melts and turns light brown. Remove from heat; add butter, stirring until butter melts.

Return mixture to low heat; gradually add half-and-half to hot mixture, 1 tablespoon at a time, stirring constantly. Cook over low heat, stirring constantly, about 3 minutes or until thickened and creamy. Stir in pecans. Yield: 1½ cups.

ORANGE DESSERT CUPS

4 navel oranges
1 cup water
½ cup sugar
¼ cup honey
2 tablespoons water
¼ cup Grand Marnier or orange juice
3 sheets frozen phyllo dough, thawed
3 tablespoons butter or margarine, melted
Frozen vanilla yogurt or ice cream

Remove rind from 2 oranges, and cut rind into thin strips. Combine strips and 1 cup water in a

Above: Cool and tangy Orange Dessert Cup turns ordinary vanilla ice cream into something special.

saucepan; bring to a boil. Reduce heat, and simmer 15 minutes. Drain, reserving strips.

Combine sugar, honey, and 2 tablespoons water in a saucepan. Bring to a boil, stirring constantly. Remove from heat, and cool.

Section oranges; drain. Combine orange sections, reserved orange rind strips, honey mixture, and Grand Marnier; stir gently. Cover and chill 8 hours.

Place 1 sheet of phyllo on a cutting board (keep remaining phyllo covered with damp towels). Lightly brush phyllo with melted butter. Layer 2 additional sheets on first sheet, brushing each with butter. Cut phyllo lengthwise into 6 strips; cut strips crosswise into thirds, forming 18 rectangles. Arrange 3 rectangles in each greased 6-ounce custard cup, forming pastry shell. Bake at 350° for 15 minutes or until golden. Remove from oven, and cool on wire racks. Remove pastry from custard cups; store in an airtight container.

Just before serving, spoon yogurt into pastry shells; top with orange mixture. Yield: 6 servings.

Above: For phyllo pastry shells, layer 3 phyllo sheets, cut lengthwise into 6 strips, and cut each strip crosswise into thirds. Arrange 3 rectangles in each 6-ounce custard cup, forming a shell.

131

To The Marvins
From The Byars

Gift Ideas

HERBED MAYONNAISE

    1   cup mayonnaise
    2   tablespoons chopped fresh parsley
    2   teaspoons freeze-dried chives
    2   teaspoons dried cilantro
    1   teaspoon grated lime rind

Combine all ingredients; spoon into an airtight container. Store in refrigerator up to 2 months. Yield: 1 cup.

Directions for gift card: Store Herbed Mayonnaise in refrigerator up to 2 months.

JEWELED PEPPER CHUTNEY

    8   large sweet red peppers, seeded and
        cut into ¼-inch cubes
    4   jalapeño peppers, finely chopped
    8   cloves garlic, minced
 2½   cups cider vinegar
    2   cups firmly packed brown sugar
    2   cups sugar
    2   cups golden raisins
    1   (2-ounce) jar crystallized ginger,
        finely chopped

Combine all ingredients in a large Dutch oven; bring to a boil. Reduce heat, and simmer, uncovered, stirring occasionally, 1 hour and 45 minutes.

Pack hot mixture into hot sterilized half-pint jars, filling to ½ inch from top. Remove air bubbles, and wipe jar rims. Cover at once with metal lids, and screw on bands. Process in boiling-water bath 10 minutes. Cool on wire racks. Yield: 6 half pints.

Directions for gift card: After opening, keep Jeweled Pepper Chutney refrigerated.

Opposite: Give a preprandial treat with Jeweled Pepper Chutney as the focus. Add purchased cheese and crackers, and package them in an interesting container—like a small galvanized bucket.

HERB MIX

    ⅓   cup dried parsley flakes
    3   tablespoons dried dillweed
    1   tablespoon freeze-dried chives
    1   teaspoon dried lemon peel
    ¼   teaspoon garlic chips
    ¼   teaspoon red pepper

Combine all ingredients. Store in an airtight container. Yield: ½ cup.

Directions for gift recipe card: For an entrée, cook 1 pound medium-size fresh shrimp, peeled and deveined, in ¼ cup melted butter over medium-high heat, stirring constantly, 3 to 4 minutes. Stir in ¼ cup white wine and 1 tablespoon Herb Mix; cover and simmer 1 minute. Serve over hot cooked rice. Yield: 3 servings.

For a salad, combine ⅓ cup white wine vinegar, ¼ cup vegetable oil, ¼ cup olive oil, and 1 tablespoon Herb Mix in a jar. Cover tightly, and shake vigorously. Serve dressing over salad greens. Yield: ¾ cup.

BRANDIED CHEESE SPREAD

    ¼   teaspoon instant coffee granules
    1   tablespoon hot water
    1   (8-ounce) package cream cheese,
        softened
    ¼   cup sugar
    2   tablespoons sour cream
    2   tablespoons brandy
    1   (2-ounce) package slivered almonds,
        toasted and chopped

Dissolve coffee granules in water in a large mixing bowl. Add cream cheese and next 3 ingredients; beat at medium speed with an electric mixer until blended. Stir in almonds. Spoon mixture into an airtight container, and refrigerate up to 1 week. Yield: 1½ cups.

Directions for gift card: Store Brandied Cheese Spread in refrigerator up to 1 week. Serve with gingersnaps or sliced apples and pears.

MUSTARD-GARLIC MARINADE

½ cup white vinegar
¼ cup dry mustard
¼ cup olive oil
2 tablespoons crushed fresh garlic
½ teaspoon salt
½ teaspoon dried tarragon
¼ teaspoon freshly ground pepper
Dash of red pepper

Combine all ingredients in a small bowl; whisk until smooth and blended. Pour mixture into a bottle; refrigerate up to 1 month. Yield: 1 cup.

Directions for gift card: Store Mustard-Garlic Marinade in refrigerator up to 1 month. Use as a marinade for firm fresh fish or pork tenderloin.

BASIL JELLY

(pictured on page 114)
1⅓ cups loosely packed fresh basil leaves
2 cups water
¾ cup white vinegar
¼ cup lemon juice
6 cups sugar
5 drops of green food coloring
1 (3-ounce) package liquid pectin

Combine first 4 ingredients in a saucepan; bring to a boil. Cover, remove from heat, and let stand 10 minutes.

Pour vinegar mixture through a wire mesh strainer into a Dutch oven, discarding leaves. Add sugar and food coloring, and bring to a boil, stirring constantly. Stir in pectin; boil 1 minute. Remove from heat, and skim off foam with a metal spoon.

Quickly pour jelly into hot sterilized jars, filling to ¼ inch from top; wipe jar rims. Cover at once with metal lids, and screw on bands. Process in boiling-water bath 5 minutes. Yield: 6 half pints.

Directions for gift card: After opening, keep Basil Jelly refrigerated.

SNOWFLAKE CUPCAKES

1 cup butter or margarine, softened
1½ cups sugar
3 large eggs
2 cups all-purpose flour
½ cup milk
1 teaspoon vanilla extract
Sifted powdered sugar

Beat butter at medium speed with an electric mixer until fluffy; gradually add sugar, beating well. Add eggs, one at a time, beating after each addition. Add flour to creamed mixture alternately with milk, beginning and ending with flour. Mix after each addition. Stir in vanilla.

Spoon batter into paper-lined miniature (1¾-inch) muffin pans, filling two-thirds full; bake at 375° for 10 to 12 minutes or until a wooden pick inserted in center comes out clean. Remove from pans, and let cool completely on wire racks. Sprinkle lightly with powdered sugar. Yield: 5 dozen.

LEMON POPPYSEED CAKES

1 (18.25-ounce) package lemon cake mix without pudding
1 (3.4-ounce) package lemon instant pudding mix
1 cup water
½ cup vegetable oil
4 large eggs
½ cup chopped pecans
1 tablespoon poppyseeds
2 tablespoons sugar
½ cup lemon juice

Combine first 5 ingredients in a large bowl; beat at medium speed with an electric mixer until blended. Stir in pecans and poppyseeds. Pour batter into three 8- x 3¾- x 2½-inch greased aluminum loafpans. Bake at 325° for 40 minutes or until a wooden pick inserted in center comes out clean, shielding with aluminum foil after 30 minutes. Cool in pans 10 minutes on wire racks.

Above: Your friends will be all set for teatime when you give them Lemon Poppyseed Cake and Russian Tea Mix. Line a basket with a napkin to hold the gifts, and add an ornament or other surprises.

Combine sugar and lemon juice; gradually brush over cakes. Let cool completely on wire racks; refrigerate up to 1 week or freeze up to 3 months. Yield: 3 loaves.

Note: Cake may be baked in a greased and floured Bundt pan. Bake at 325° for 1 hour or until a wooden pick inserted in center comes out clean, shielding with aluminum foil after 45 minutes. Cool in pan on a wire rack 10 minutes; remove from pan. Gradually brush with lemon mixture. Let cool completely on a wire rack.

RUSSIAN TEA MIX

  2 **cups orange-flavored breakfast**
     beverage crystals
  1 **to 1¼ cups sugar**
  ½ **cup instant tea**
  2 **(0.31-ounce) packages unsweetened**
     lemonade-flavored drink mix
  1 **teaspoon ground cinnamon**
  ½ **teaspoon ground cloves**

Combine all ingredients; store mixture in an airtight container. Yield: 3¾ cups.

  Directions for gift recipe card: Stir Russian Tea Mix before using. Combine 1 tablespoon plus 1 teaspoon tea mix with 1 cup hot water.

Above: Offer a do-it-yourself dessert with Chocolate Chip Pie Mix, packaged in a decorative take-out box. Add flavored coffee, paper napkins, and perhaps a wooden scoop, and present them in a towel-lined basket.

CHOCOLATE CHIP PIE MIX

1 cup sugar
½ cup all-purpose flour
1 (6-ounce) package semisweet
 chocolate morsels
½ cup flaked coconut
½ cup chopped pecans

Combine sugar and flour; place in an airtight plastic bag. Tie with ribbon and label "Dry ingredients." Place chocolate morsels, coconut, and pecans in a second airtight plastic bag; tie with ribbon and label "Chocolate packet." Place both bags in a decorated box or colorful bag tied with ribbon. Yield: One 2-bag gift.

Directions for gift recipe card: Combine ¼ cup melted butter or margarine, dry ingredient packet, and 2 large eggs; stir until dry ingredients are moistened. Stir in chocolate packet, and spoon mixture into a 9-inch pastry shell. Bake at 350° for 35 to 40 minutes. Yield: one 9-inch pie.

PUMPKIN BUTTER

1 (16-ounce) can cooked, mashed
 pumpkin
3 tablespoons powdered fruit
 pectin
1 teaspoon ground cinnamon
½ teaspoon ground allspice
2 ¼ cups sugar

Combine all ingredients in a heavy saucepan; bring to a boil over medium heat, stirring constantly. Boil 1 minute, stirring constantly; remove from heat, and let cool. Spoon into three 1-cup gift containers; refrigerate up to 3 weeks or freeze up to 3 months. Yield: 3 cups.

Microwave Directions: Combine first 4 ingredients in a 2-quart glass bowl. Microwave at HIGH 6 minutes, stirring at 2-minute intervals. Stir in sugar, and microwave at HIGH 8 to 10 minutes or until mixture comes to a boil, stirring once. Microwave at HIGH 1 minute; let cool. Spoon mixture into three 1-cup gift containers;

Above: Team up Pumpkin Butter with purchased muffins, wrapped in doilies for a prettier presentation. Scout flea markets for unusual containers such as wire baskets or china bowls to hold the gifts.

refrigerate up to 3 weeks or freeze up to 3 months.

Directions for gift card: Store Pumpkin Butter in refrigerator up to 3 weeks or in freezer up to 3 months.

Gifts Kids Can Make

WHITE CHOCOLATE CRUNCH

1. pound vanilla-flavored candy coating
2. cups tiny pretzels
3. (3-ounce) packages salted peanuts
4. cup corn-and-rice cereal

Above: Making food gifts is a good way to let children help in the family gift-giving. These recipes are delicious, and easy enough for young cooks.

Trace a 10-inch circle on wax paper. Turn paper over and place on baking sheet; set aside.

Place candy coating in a 2-quart glass bowl; microwave at MEDIUM (50% power) 5 minutes or until melted, stirring after 3 minutes. Stir in pretzels and remaining ingredients. Spoon mixture into center of prepared circle, spreading to edge; let cool. Remove wax paper and cover with plastic wrap. Yield: 1½ pounds.

Note: Package candy for gift-giving by placing on a 10-inch cake board; cover with plastic wrap and tie with ribbon.

SHORTCUT GINGERBREAD COOKIES

1. (18.25-ounce) package spice cake mix
2. teaspoon ground ginger
¼ cup vegetable oil
2. large eggs
¼ cup molasses

Combine cake mix and ginger in a large bowl; add oil, eggs, and molasses, stirring until blended. Shape dough into a ball; wrap in wax paper, and chill 2 hours.

Knead dough on a floured surface; roll to ¼-inch thickness, rolling dough between 2 pieces of wax paper on a cookie sheet. Remove top paper, and place 4-inch gift tags on top of dough; using a table knife, cut around designs. Freeze 5 minutes or until firm. Lift cutouts off with a spatula, and place on ungreased cookie sheets. (Reroll excess dough.) Bake at 375° for 9 to 10 minutes. Cool 2 to 3 minutes before removing from cookie sheet; cool on wire racks. Top each cookie with a matching gift tag; cover completely with plastic wrap. Yield: 21 cookies.

EDIBLE ORNAMENTS

¼ cup butter or margarine,
    softened
⅓ cup light corn syrup
1   teaspoon vanilla extract
1   (16-ounce) package powdered sugar
    Green food coloring
    Red cinnamon candies
1   (4¼-ounce) tube white decorating
    frosting

Combine first 3 ingredients in a large mixing
bowl; beat at medium speed with an electric mixer
until blended. Gradually add half of powdered
sugar, beating until smooth. Stir in enough remaining powdered sugar to make a stiff dough,
kneading with hands, if necessary. Divide dough
in half; wrap one portion in plastic wrap and set
aside.

To make wreaths, knead green food coloring
into half of dough, and shape into 18 (1-inch)
balls. Roll each ball into a 5-inch rope and connect ends to form a circle; decorate with candies.

To make cutout ornaments, roll out remaining
dough on a surface lightly dusted with powdered
sugar. Using 3-inch cookie cutters, cut into

desired shapes. Using a drinking straw, make a
hole in top of each ornament. Decorate with
frosting.

Let ornaments partially dry, uncovered, on wax
paper 4 hours. Remove from wax paper and transfer to wire racks; let dry 24 hours. To hang, tie
with ribbon. Yield: about 3 dozen ornaments.

Note: Make these ornaments four weeks before
Christmas to give as early gifts. Thread with colorful ribbon so they're ready to hang.

SNACK MIX

1   (15-ounce) package raisins
1   (16-ounce) jar dry roasted
    peanuts
1   (12-ounce) package butterscotch or
    peanut butter morsels
1   (1½-ounce) package milk chocolate
    morsels

Combine all ingredients; store in an airtight container. Yield: 10 cups.

*Above: Making Christmas ornament cookies is
child's play. Your children will be thrilled that these
special gifts are their own handiwork.*

BROWN SUGAR BROWNIE MIX

1   (16-ounce) package dark brown
    sugar
2   cups self-rising flour
½   cup chopped pecans

Combine all ingredients; store in a heavy-duty,
zip-top plastic bag. Yield: 1 gift package.
Directions for gift recipe card: Combine
Brown Sugar Brownie Mix and 4 large eggs, stirring until blended. Spoon into a greased 13- x 9-
x 2-inch pan. Bake at 350° for 25 to 28 minutes.
Cool and cut into squares. Yield: 4 dozen.

Note: To make Brown Sugar Brownie Mix as
much fun for a child to *receive* as to make, put the
gift package in a plastic sand pail with a shovel.
The pail and shovel are ideal for mixing up the
brownies and will be fun for the beach later.

Patterns
Emboss Copper for
Starry Frames

Instructions are on page 70.
Patterns are full-size.

SMALL PICTURE FRAME

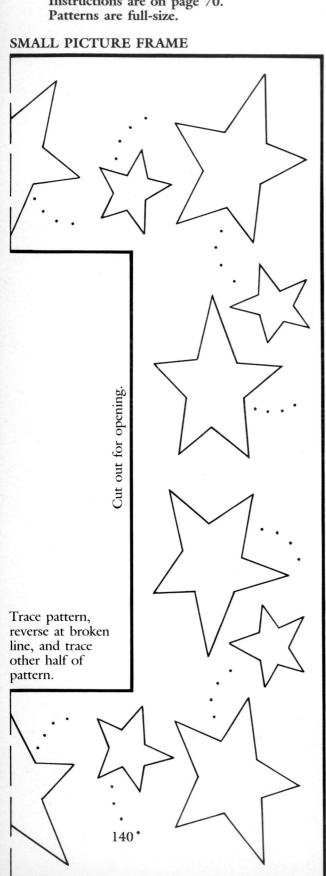

Cut out for opening.

Trace pattern,
reverse at broken
line, and trace
other half of
pattern.

140

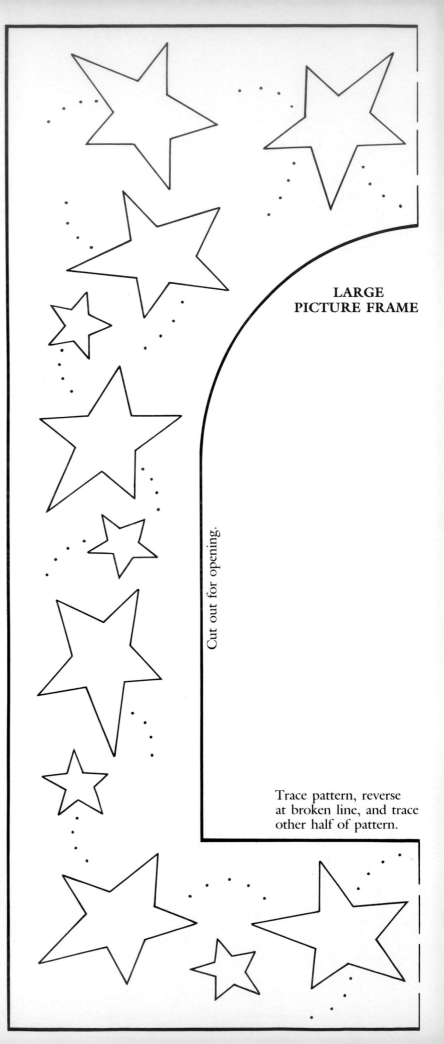

**LARGE
PICTURE FRAME**

Cut out for opening.

Trace pattern, reverse
at broken line, and trace
other half of pattern.

A Coppery Christmas

SPONGED COPPER TREE
Instructions are on page 72.
Pattern is full-size.

ROUND EMBOSSED ORNAMENT
Instructions are on page 73.
Pattern is full-size.

Center line: Trace pattern, reverse at broken line, and trace other half of pattern.

Cutting line

141

Wise Men from Wood

Instructions are on pages 78-79.
Patterns are full-size.

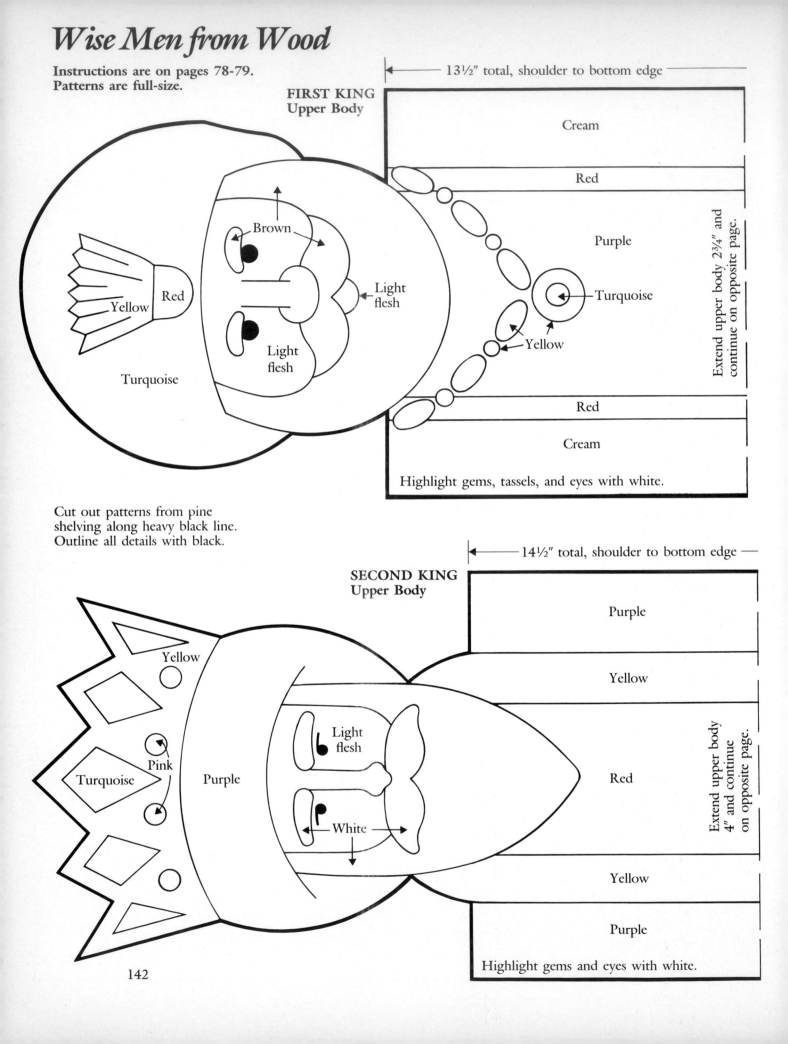

FIRST KING
Upper Body

13½″ total, shoulder to bottom edge

Cream

Red

Purple

Turquoise

Yellow

Extend upper body 2¾″ and continue on opposite page.

Red

Cream

Highlight gems, tassels, and eyes with white.

Brown

Light flesh

Light flesh

Yellow

Red

Turquoise

Cut out patterns from pine shelving along heavy black line. Outline all details with black.

SECOND KING
Upper Body

14½″ total, shoulder to bottom edge

Purple

Yellow

Red

Yellow

Purple

Extend upper body 4″ and continue on opposite page.

Highlight gems and eyes with white.

Yellow

Turquoise

Pink

Purple

Light flesh

White

142

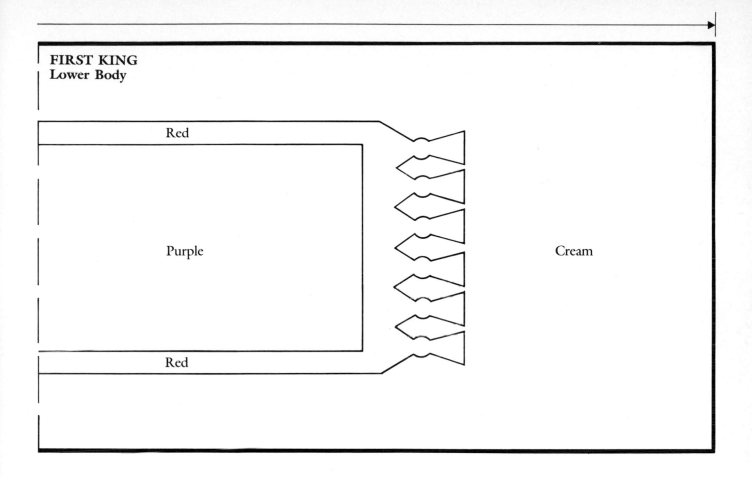

FIRST KING
Lower Body

Red

Purple

Cream

Red

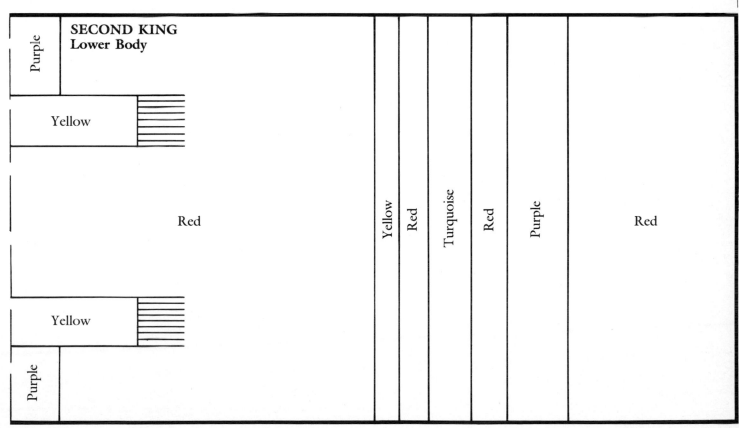

Purple

SECOND KING
Lower Body

Yellow

Red

Yellow

Purple

Yellow

Red

Turquoise

Red

Purple

Red

Wise Men from Wood
CONTINUED

Instructions are on pages 78-79.
Patterns are full-size.
Cut out pattern along heavy black line.
Outline all details with black.

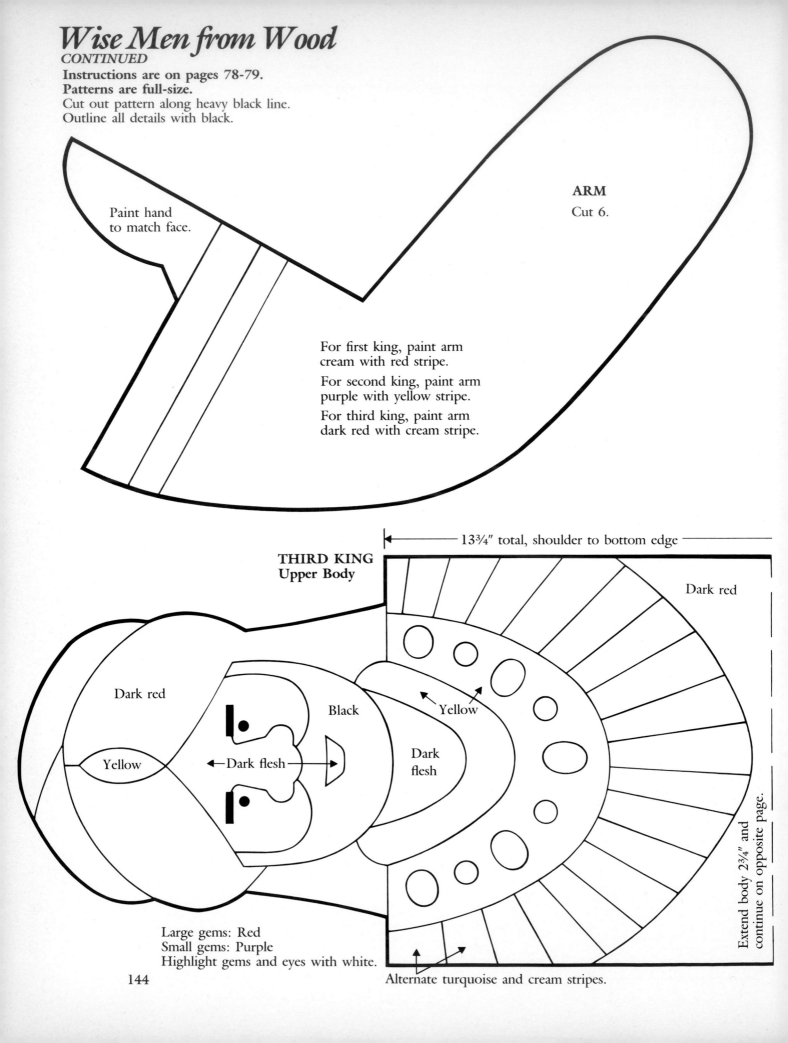

Paint hand
to match face.

ARM
Cut 6.

For first king, paint arm
cream with red stripe.

For second king, paint arm
purple with yellow stripe.

For third king, paint arm
dark red with cream stripe.

13¾″ total, shoulder to bottom edge

THIRD KING
Upper Body

Dark red

Dark red

Black

Yellow

Dark red

Yellow

Dark
flesh

Dark flesh

Extend body 2¾″ and
continue on opposite page.

Large gems: Red
Small gems: Purple
Highlight gems and eyes with white.

144

Alternate turquoise and cream stripes.

FRENCH HORN NAPKIN MOTIF
Instructions are on page 60.
Pattern is full-size.

THIRD KING Lower Body				
Dark red	Pink	Red	Pink	Purple
				Turquoise
				Purple
				Turquoise
				Purple
				Turquoise
				Purple
				Turquoise

145

Appliqué a Reindeer Stocking

**Instructions are on page 81.
Patterns are full-size.**

Cut appliqué pieces along heavy solid lines.

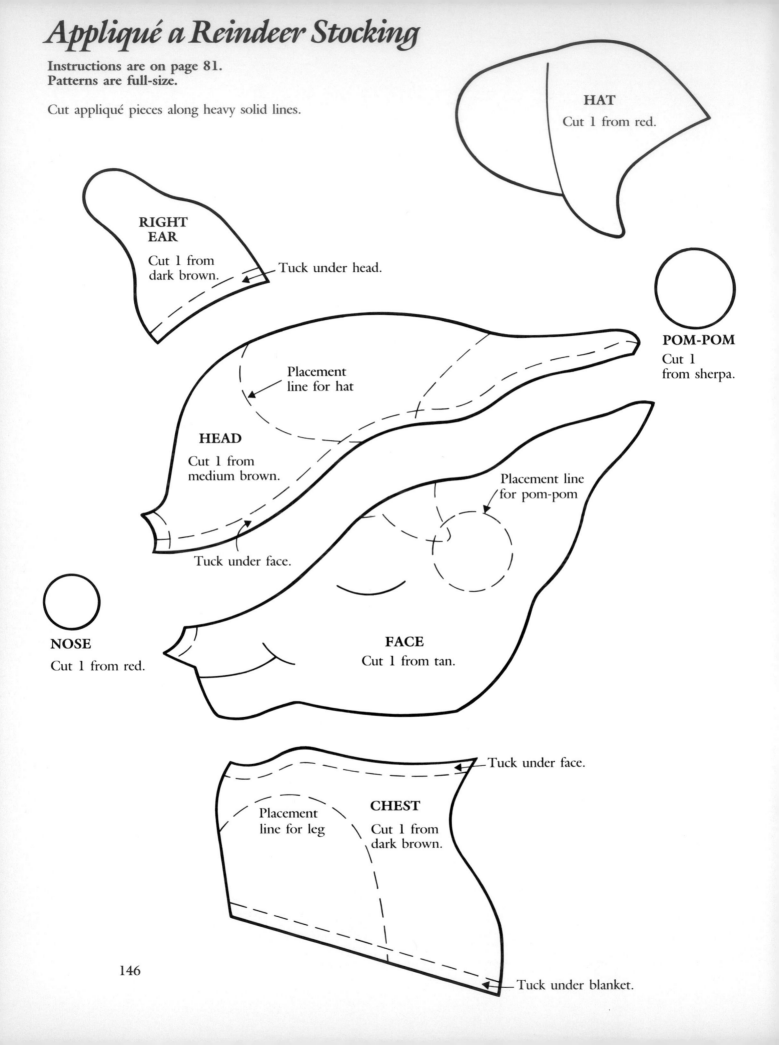

HAT
Cut 1 from red.

**RIGHT
EAR**

Cut 1 from
dark brown.

— Tuck under head.

POM-POM
Cut 1
from sherpa.

Placement
line for hat

HEAD

Cut 1 from
medium brown.

Placement line
for pom-pom

Tuck under face.

NOSE

Cut 1 from red.

FACE
Cut 1 from tan.

Tuck under face.

Placement
line for leg

CHEST

Cut 1 from
dark brown.

146

Tuck under blanket.

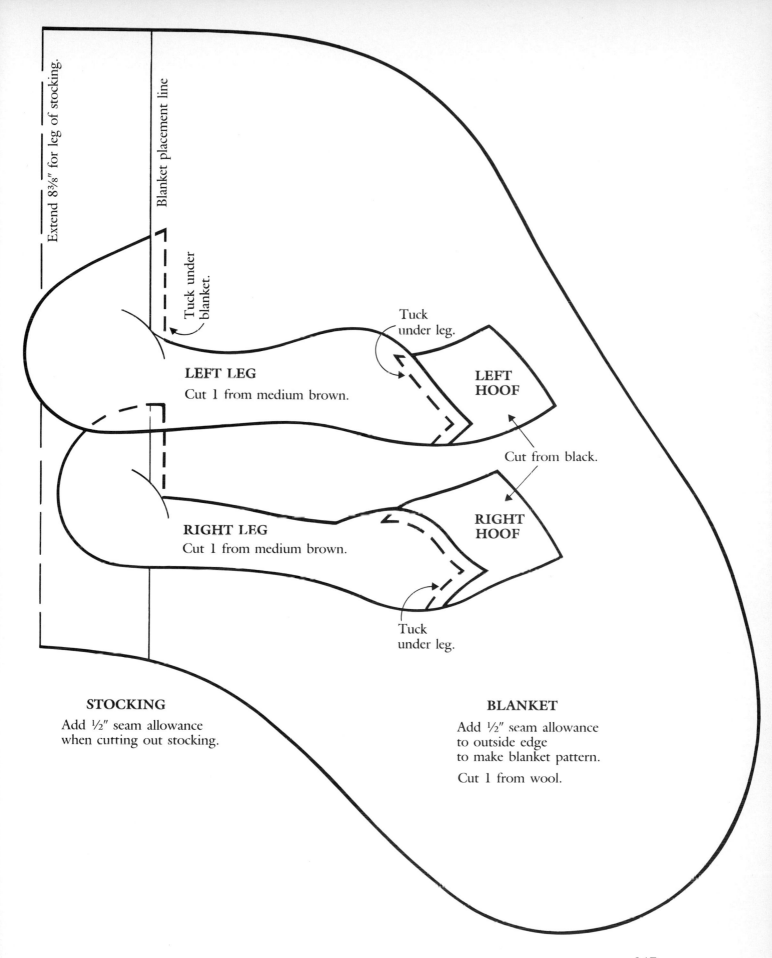

Extend 8³⁄₈″ for leg of stocking.

Blanket placement line

Tuck under blanket.

Tuck under leg.

LEFT LEG

Cut 1 from medium brown.

LEFT HOOF

Cut from black.

RIGHT LEG

Cut 1 from medium brown.

RIGHT HOOF

Tuck under leg.

STOCKING

Add ½″ seam allowance when cutting out stocking.

BLANKET

Add ½″ seam allowance to outside edge to make blanket pattern.

Cut 1 from wool.

Bunny on the Moon

Instructions are on page 74.
Patterns are full-size.

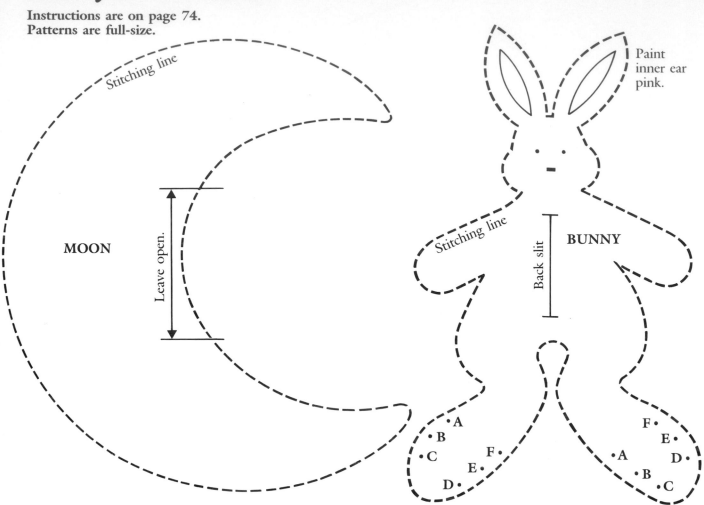

Stitching line

MOON

Leave open.

Paint inner ear pink.

Stitching line

Back slit

BUNNY

·A
·B
·C
·F
·E
·D

F·
·E
·A
·D
·B
·C

Beaded Stained-Glass Ornaments

Instructions are on page 85.

Cross-stitch Charts

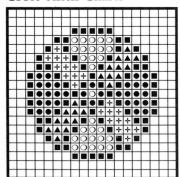

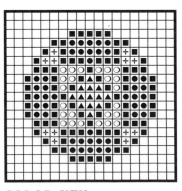

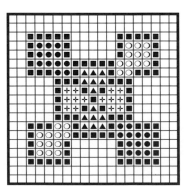

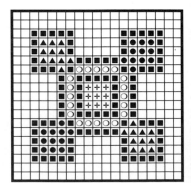

Use doubled quilting thread to attach beads.

COLOR KEY
(for beads):

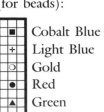

■ Cobalt Blue
+ Light Blue
○ Gold
● Red
▲ Green

Woven-Ribbon Cookie Tins

Instructions are on page 87.

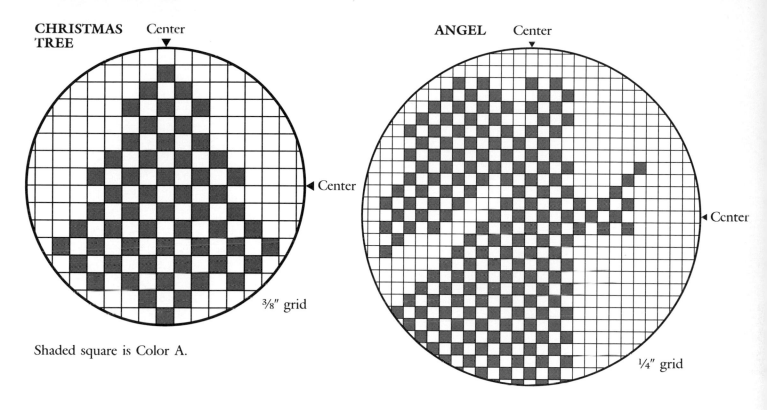

CHRISTMAS TREE Center

◄ Center

⅜" grid

Shaded square is Color A.

ANGEL Center

◄ Center

¼" grid

Beaded Ornaments,
continued

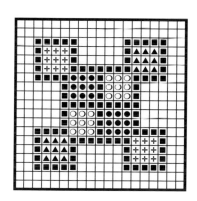

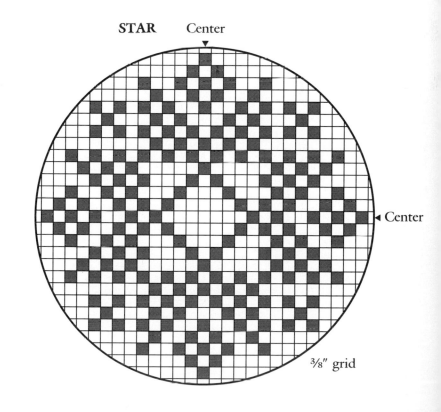

STAR Center

◄ Center

⅜" grid

Perfect Pines on Hearts and Squares

PINE TREE HEART POCKET
Instructions are on page 89.
Pattern is full-size and
includes ¼″ seam allowance.

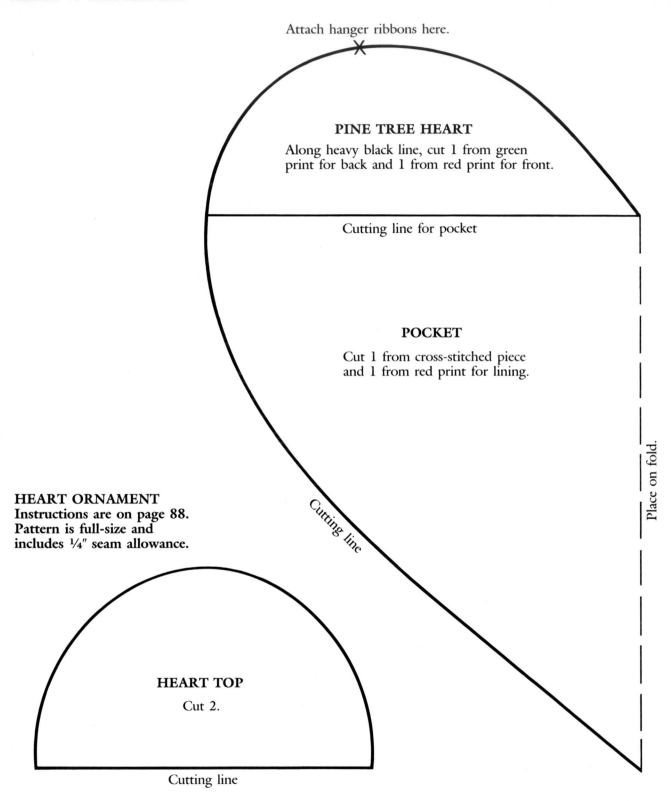

Attach hanger ribbons here.

PINE TREE HEART

Along heavy black line, cut 1 from green
print for back and 1 from red print for front.

Cutting line for pocket

POCKET

Cut 1 from cross-stitched piece
and 1 from red print for lining.

Cutting line

Place on fold.

HEART ORNAMENT
Instructions are on page 88.
Pattern is full-size and
includes ¼″ seam allowance.

HEART TOP

Cut 2.

Cutting line

Pine Tree Heart Pocket
Cross-stitch Chart

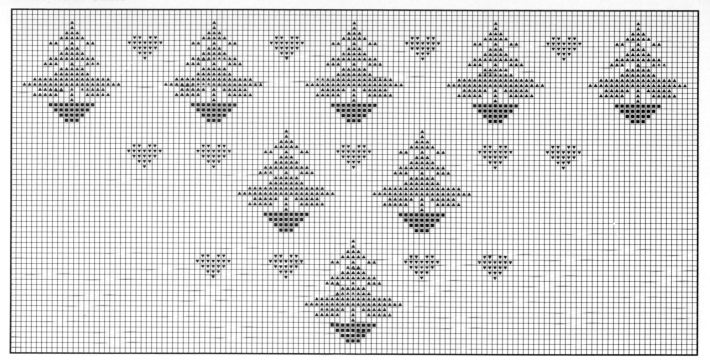

COLOR KEY
(*Note*: Numbers are for DMC floss.)
Use **2** strands for all stitching.

- ▲ 319 Green
- ♥ 816 Red
- ■ 310 Black

Ornament
Cross-stitch Chart

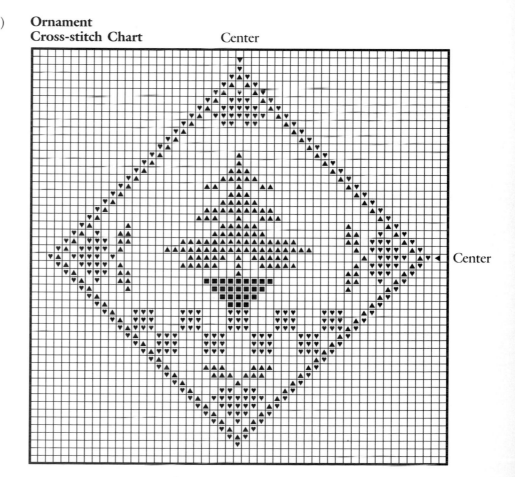

Center

◄ Center

Punched-Paper Card

Instructions are on page 96.
Pattern is full-size.

Size of dot indicates size of pinhole.

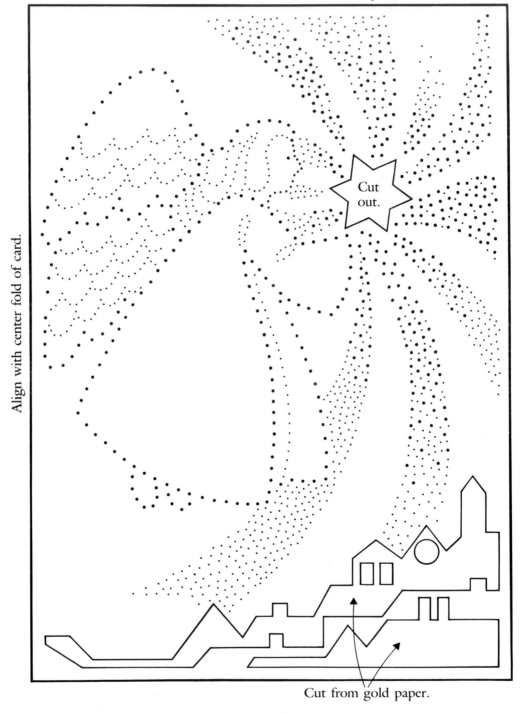

Align with center fold of card.

Cut
out.

Cut from gold paper.

Eskimo Sweater and Earmuffs

Instructions are on page 94.
Patterns are full-size.

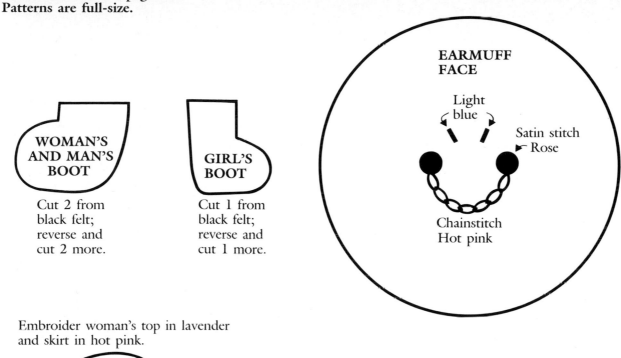

WOMAN'S AND MAN'S BOOT

Cut 2 from black felt; reverse and cut 2 more.

GIRL'S BOOT

Cut 1 from black felt; reverse and cut 1 more.

EARMUFF FACE

Light blue

Satin stitch
Rose

Chainstitch
Hot pink

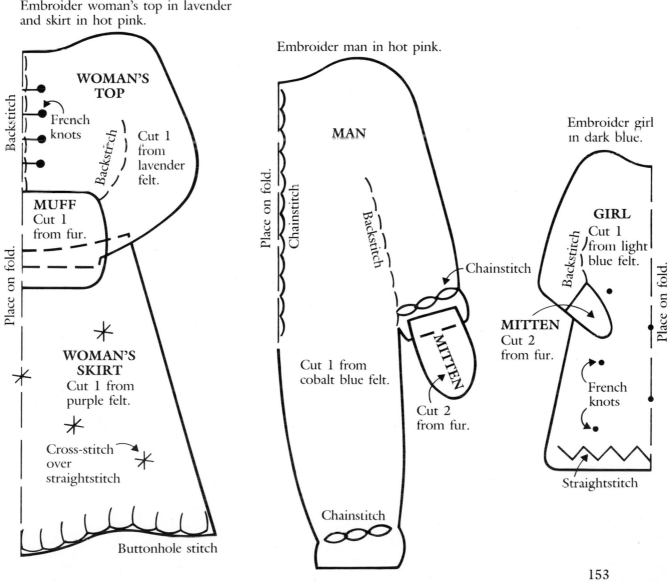

Embroider woman's top in lavender and skirt in hot pink.

Embroider man in hot pink.

Embroider girl in dark blue.

WOMAN'S TOP

Backstitch

French knots

Backstitch

Cut 1 from lavender felt.

MUFF
Cut 1 from fur.

Place on fold.

WOMAN'S SKIRT

Cut 1 from purple felt.

Cross-stitch over straightstitch

Buttonhole stitch

MAN

Place on fold.

Chainstitch

Backstitch

Chainstitch

Cut 1 from cobalt blue felt.

MITTEN

Cut 2 from fur.

Chainstitch

GIRL

Cut 1 from light blue felt.

Backstitch

MITTEN
Cut 2 from fur.

Place on fold.

French knots

Straightstitch

The Chrismon Tradition

Cross-stitch and Crochet Charts
Instructions are on pages 41 and 42.

COLOR KEY FOR CROSS-STITCH
Use 3 strands for all cross-stitching.

	White
*	743 Gold (DMC floss)

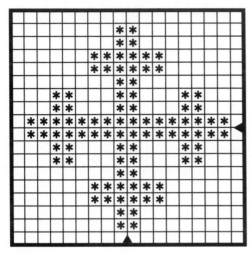

CROSS CROSSLET
4 Latin crosses joined at the base to
symbolize the spread of the Christian
message through all the world

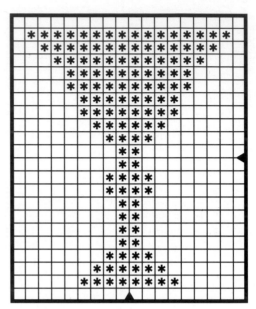

CHALICE
Communion

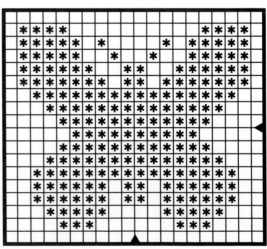

5-POINT STAR
Epiphany

BUTTERFLY
Resurrection and eternal life

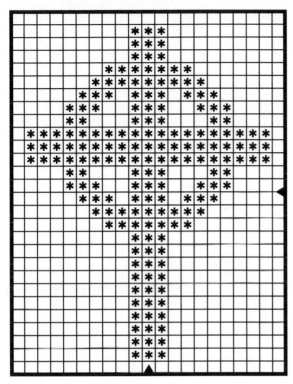

CELTIC CROSS
Ancient symbol combining a circle (eternity and the Trinity) and the cross (Crucifixion)

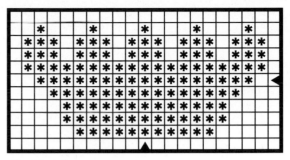

CROWN
Kingship, victory over sin and death

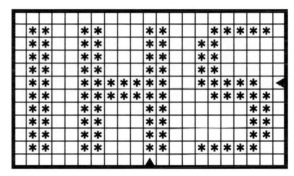

MONOGRAM
The first 3 letters of the Greek spelling of Jesus

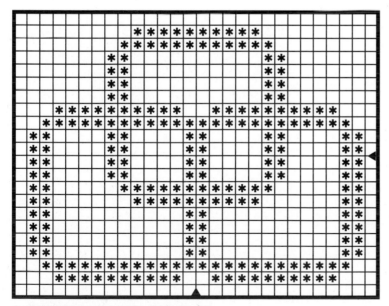

3 INTERTWINING CIRCLES
The Trinity

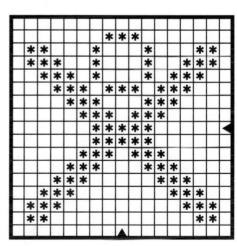

BABY IN CRIB
The Nativity

Contributors

DESIGNERS

Barbara Ball, woven-ribbon cookie tins, 86-87; punched-paper card, 96.

Catherine S. Corbett, decoupage clay pot, 76-77.

Susan Z. Douglas, crocheted star garland, 68; knitted kitties, 82-84; crocheted tree skirt and stocking, 90-93.

Howard C. Eckhart, gold lamé roses, 59.

Vicki Ingham, French horn napkins, 60; brass-and-copper wire wreath, 73; round embossed ornament, 73.

Larry Janzen, mantel arrangement, 6; dining table, 7.

Heidi T. King, copper place cards and napkin rings, 64; recycled cards, 76-77; Eskimo sweater and earmuffs, 94-95.

Jo S. Kittinger, appliqué stocking, 81.

Carol Krob, beaded ornaments, 85.

Margaret Allen Northen, Chrismons, 41-42.

Rosemary Rae Sterling, moon bunny ornament, 74-75.

Katie Stoddard, marbleized place mats, napkin rings, and candle shades, 59; copper candlesticks, 63; sponged copper tree, 72.

Carol M. Tipton, copper picture frames, 70-71; wooden Wise Men, 78-79.

Suzanne Wall, pine tree ornaments and heart pocket, 88-89.

Dianne West, Sculpey carolers, 80.

Grady Wheeler, door decoration, 44.

PHOTOGRAPHERS

All photographs by **John O'Hagan** except the following:

Hal Lott, 4, 5, 6, 7, 8, 9, 23, 24, 26, 27, 28, 29, 32, 33, 46, 47, 54, 55, 56, 57, 67.

Sylvia Martin, 10, 11, 12, 13, 34, 35, 36, 38, 39, 65.

Gary Clark, 20, 21 bottom, 22 top, 80, 89.

Beth Maynor, 21 top, 22 bottom, 30, 31, 50, 51, 52.

Melissa Springer, 37, 40.

Mary-Gray Hunter, 41, 42, 66, 76, 77, 86, 95, 96, 97.

Charles Walton, 108, 111, 112, 113, 114, 118, 125, 132, 135, 136, 137.

Colleen Duffley, 99, 100, 101, 102-103, 104, 107, 119, 122-23, 126, 131, 138, 139.

PHOTOSTYLISTS

All photostyling by **Katie Stoddard** except the following:

Leslie Byars, 99, 100, 102-103, 104, 107, 108, 111, 112, 113, 114, 118, 119, 122-23, 125, 126, 131, 132, 135, 136, 137, 138, 139.

Joetta Moulden, 4, 5, 6, 7, 8, 9, 26, 27, 28, 29, 32, 33, 46, 47, 54, 55, 56, 57, 67.

Special thanks to the *Southern Living* Test Kitchens staff for preparing recipes.

ACKNOWLEDGMENTS

Card for jigsaw puzzle greeting on page 77, courtesy of Mary Engelbreit & Sunrise Publications.

Our thanks to Bromberg and Co., Inc., for the use of crystal and china for "Terrific Tablescapes," to Homewood Musical Instrument Co. for the use of a French horn, and to Fitz and Floyd for props used in "Celebrations from the Kitchen."

RESOURCES

For mail-order sources of earmuff frames (page 94) and paste food coloring (page 119), please write to *Christmas with Southern Living 1992*, Oxmoor House, 2100 Lakeshore Drive, Birmingham, AL 35209.